R00492 98226

BROADWAY PLAY PUBLISHING, INC.

TM

CHICAGO PUBLIC LIBRARY
HAROLD WASHINGTON LIBRARY CENTER

R0049298226

Death in the Pot

by

Manuel Van Loggem

249 WEST 29 STREET NEW YORK NY 10001 (212) 563-3820

DEATH IN THE POT

Copyright © 1983 by Manuel Van Loggem

All rights reserved. This work is fully protected under the copyright law of the United States of America.

No part of this publication may be photocopied, reproduced, stored in a retrieval system, or transmitted, in any form or by any means, electronic, mechanical, recording or otherwise without the prior permission of the publisher. Additional copies of this edition are available from the publisher.

Written permission is required for live performance of any sort. This includes readings, cuttings, scenes and excerpts. For amateur and stock performance, please contact Broadway Play Publishing, Inc.

For all other rights please contact Manuel Van Loggem, Nieuwe Keizersgracht 59, 1018 VC Amsterdam, The Netherlands.

First printing: January 1983

ISBN: 0-88145-000-6

Cover art by Craig Nealy.
Design by Marie Donovan.
Set in Baskerville by BakerSmith Type, NYC.
Printed and bound by BookCrafters, Inc., Chelsea MI.

REF
PR
9130.9
.L6
D4
1983
K00492 98226

MANUEL VAN LOGGEM was born in Amsterdam, the Netherlands, where he is still living. Besides being a psychologist (he
graduated in 1955 from the University of Amsterdam and
specialized in psychotherapy), he is a writer of novels, short
stories and plays (for the stage, TV and radio). He has also
written six books on the theory of drama, including THE
PSYCHOLOGY OF DRAMA.

A SELECTION OF HIS PUBLISHED NOVELS:

A trilogy about the history of the Jews, as reflected in the
three great religious leaders who have shaped the history of
Western civilization.

1. MOSES, now in its fourth printing, was published in 1946.

2. A JEW FROM NAZARETH. A historical novel about the leader
of a small Jewish baptist sect who, through the work of Paul,
became a God of Christianity. (Published in 1980)

3. A JEW FROM TARSUS. The life of the founder of Christianity,
Paul, who also laid the foundations for religious anti-Semitism.
(Due in December 1982)

A SUN ON HIROSHIMA, a short novel about the man who was
involved in the preparation of the attack on Nagasaki and
Hiroshima and who, after his return to the USA, drifted into
a life of petty crimes and ended up in a mental hospital. (Two
printings in 1963) The book describes the mental anguish of
a man who suffered from unbearable feelings of guilt and
tried to atone for his deed.

THE CHARNEL CROSS, a pirates' novel, was published in Dutch
in 1968 and entirely rewritten in English in 1982.

DEATH IN THE POT, a detective novel, will be published in
March 1983.

COLLECTIONS OF SHORT STORIES

INSECTS IN PLASTIC, a novelette about the mechanisms of
brainwashing in a totalitarian state. It was awarded the impor-

tant *Bookweek* Award in 1952. Reprinted four times (Sale: 200,000).

PAIRPUPPETS (1974). A collection of science-fiction stories. Van Loggem is considered one of the main writers of SF in the Netherlands.

NEW WORLDS FROM THE LOWLANDS. An anthology of Dutch SF and fantasy, with an introduction and contribution by van Loggem. (1982: Printed in the USA) Preface by Isaac Asimov.

PRODUCED PLAYS

KILL THE PIGS (3 young male characters, 1 female) One setting. The psychological background of a juvenile gang murder. (Produced in Holland, Belgium, Switzerland, Germany, Finland, Sweden)

THE TIME OF THE COFFINS. (Produced in Holland) A play about suicide in a welfare state. Black comedy in which the taking of one's own life is a class prerogative. (3 men, 2 women, one setting)

A SUN ON HIROSHIMA. (Produced in Holland) Adaptation of the short novel of the same title. See description under *Published Novels*. (4 characters in changing parts)

OEDIPUS IN THE SUBURB. (Produced in Holland) A play about a modern Yocaste and her son Oedipus (Eddy). He has sexual relations with his mother, kills his father in a car accident and when the truth comes out Yoke does *not* kill herself and Eddy does not stab out his eyes. After the revelation by Cora (the Choir, a social worker), they live happily thereafter. (2 men, 2 women, one setting)

ACCIDENTS ARE HUMAN. A comedy. (3 men, 3 women) (Produced in the USA at the Guggenheim Summer Theatre, New Jersey).

For his entire dramatic works Van Loggem received the prestigious Edmund Hustinx Award in 1978.

CHARACTERS

JEANNE HAREWOOD .... the professor's wife
ALBERT WESTER .... a friend of the family
EWALD HAREWOOD .... a professor of Mycology
HELEN ENGELS .... his secretary
A COMMERCIAL TRAVELLER
INSPECTOR VERMONT

The scene is laid in the professor's study.

II Kings 4:38-40. Elisha returned to Gilgal at a time when there was a famine in the land. One day, when a group of prophets was sitting at his feet, he said to his servant: "Set the big pot on the fire and prepare some broth for the company." One of them went into the fields to gather herbs and found a wild vine, and filled the skirt of his garment with bitter-apples. He came back and sliced them into the pot, not knowing what they were. They poured it out for the men to eat, but, when they tasted it, they cried out: "Man of God, there is death in the pot," and they could not eat it.

Act One

(The study belonging to EWALD HAREWOOD, *Professor of Mycology, the science of mushrooms. When the curtain rises, his wife* JEANNE *is seen snooping about the room. She listens attentively, then takes a small bottle from a shelf. She starts and puts the bottle back. She then goes to the bookcase and takes, from a row of imposing books, a bottle of whisky and a glass. She pours herself a drink, puts the bottle back and drinks with obvious relish. She takes another drink, it does her a lot of good. She then cleans the glass. She is still cleaning it, when she hears sounds from outside. Frightened, she hastily puts the glass back behind the books. A moment later* ALBERT WESTER *enters. He is younger than* JEANNE.*)*

ALBERT: Did I scare you?

JEANNE: Me? No.

ALBERT: I thought I did.

JEANNE: No. why should I be scared?

ALBERT: I don't know. I thought I saw you jump.

JEANNE: I'm quite all right.

ALBERT: So I was wrong. Let's not make a point about it. I'm a pretty easy guy. When people say something, I usually take their words for it.

JEANNE: What are you doing here?

ALBERT: I'm looking for a book.

JEANNE: I didn't know you could read.

ALBERT:*(Sharply)*
I don't like that kind of remark.

JEANNE: You should've invented something more convincing.

ALBERT: I like the view here better than anywhere else in the house. So I came to admire it.

JEANNE: Does Ewald know that you snoop around his study when he's not there?

ALBERT: Ewald and I are friends. His room is my room. *(Looks around)*
It's an awful mess here. I don't know how he can ever find anything.

JEANNE: He's a professor. They're always a bit absent-minded.

ALBERT: You should tidy up the place a bit.

JEANNE: Ewald doesn't like that

ALBERT: I can imagine.

JEANNE: Why?

ALBERT: What?

JEANNE: Why can you imagine he doesn't like it when I tidy up?

ALBERT: Did I say that?

JEANNE: You did.

ALBERT: Well, I just imagined it.

JEANNE: You never just imagine something.

ALBERT: You seem to know a lot about me.

JEANNE: Yes. I do. I've got to know you.

ALBERT: You think you can look through me, eh?

JEANNE: That's right.

ALBERT: You could be terribly mistaken.

JEANNE: No, I'm not mistaken. I know you.

ALBERT: Sometimes I'd like to smack you right in the middle of that upper middle class mug of yours. I don't like the way you talk. You think you're too good for me, don't you?

JEANNE: No, I don't.

ALBERT: Then don't be so high-faluting.

JEANNE: It's because I've been born and bred with it. The way you talk is always the last to go. *(Kisses him)* Don't be so sour.

ALBERT: It's all right. *(Embraces her in a casual way)* That better?

JEANNE: Yes, that's better. *(She starts)*

ALBERT: What is it?

JEANNE: I thought I heard something.

ALBERT: *(Listens)* No. It's your imagination.

JEANNE: *(Continues tidying the room)* The carelessness of that man is criminal. *(Takes a bottle from a shelf)* This is pure poison. Extract of mushrooms.

ALBERT: You couldn't tell by the color. Just looks like weak tea.

JEANNE: It's not the color that does it.

ALBERT: He knows how to handle that stuff. It's his job. What's that funny name they call him again?

JEANNE: Mycologist.

ALBERT: Obscene. Mycologist. What does it mean exactly?

JEANNE: That he knows all there is to know about mushrooms.

ALBERT: What funny hobbies people have. They made him a Professor because of all that trash?

JEANNE: Yes. He must be very smart. One of the best in the profession. I've been told he's world-famous, but he never talks to me about his work.

ALBERT: And they pay him for it?

JEANNE: Yes.

ALBERT: Much?

JEANNE: What do you mean?

ALBERT: Do they pay him much for that kind of work?

JEANNE: He's a Professor.

ALBERT: A man like him hasn't got much to spend on pleasure, of course.

JEANNE: He buys a lot of books.

ALBERT: *(Goes to the bookcase)* What a waste of money. I've been told that there are books that cost more than two bottles of rye.

JEANNE: Some even more than three.

ALBERT: Tut-tut.

JEANNE: *(Puts the bottle away)* One drop of that stuff would be enough.

ALBERT: *(Reflectively)* Yes. *(Sighs)* No. Definitely not.

JEANNE: What do you mean?

ALBERT: A person might think, one drop, that's not too much. One drop in the coffee or in the spinach, and you solve a lot of problems. But it can't be done. Trust the word of a man who knows more about this kind of thing than you do. It can't be done. That husband of yours, he's not that old yet, is he? Fortyish?

JEANNE: Yes.

ALBERT: When a man like that suddenly dies, doctors have the habit of getting suspicious. That's how they are made. They get suspicious and they begin to investigate: that's a dirty job. They cut up everything. Heart, liver, stomach, lungs. Autopsy, they call it. Then it turns out that the man has met his end in an unnatural way, which makes them think. And when doctors start thinking you better make yourself scarce 'cause you can be sure that nasty things are going to happen. Now Albert really does like a good life, but he's also very careful. Albert never takes risks.

JEANNE: *(Looks again at the bottle)* You could make it look like an accident. He's really very careless.

ALBERT: Think of the fingerprints. (ALBERT *gives her his hand-kerchief. She wipes the bottle and puts it away.)*

JEANNE: Yes, you could make it look like an accident.

ALBERT: Those doctors, of course, go to the police. That's their duty as law-abiding citizens. You can't even blame them. The police send an inspector who begins to inspect. He puts his nose into all sorts of things. He ferrets out, for instance, that a nice young fellow—that's me—was a friend of the family and that the Professor, how shall I put it, lived in quiet disharmony with his wife; have I said it decently enough?

JEANNE: They'd have to prove it.

ALBERT: Don't underestimate them. And then there's the insurance company. How much?

JEANNE: Fifty thousand pounds.

ALBERT: That's a lot. That's a helluva lot for a dry and stuffy old mushroom professor. To look at him you wouldn't think he was worth that much.

JEANNE: Alive he isn't.

ALBERT: No, that's true. I forgot. He's only worth fifty thousand pounds if he's dead.

JEANNE: Yes. It's a pity.

ALBERT: *(Looks at the rows of bottles, visibly reflecting. Finally he turns, resolutely)* Leave everything to me.

JEANNE: But we can't go on this way.

ALBERT: I'll think it over. I'm sure I'll manage to cook up something. But remember, keep your fingers out. *(She says nothing and he looks at her reflectively)* You hear me? I don't want you to spoil the whole performance with your dumb tricks. You have no more brains in that silly head of yours than a chicken. I'm sure I'll find a way. We have time to think of something nice, something beautiful, without having to take any risks. It's just a matter of using the old thinking machine in the right way to get the best results. I even believe I've got hold of something already.

JEANNE: What?

ALBERT: Something that might prove to be very useful. Don't ask me what. I'll tell you in time.

JEANNE: We haven't got that much time.

ALBERT: Plenty of time.

JEANNE: He must have noticed something. He *must* have.

ALBERT: It's not as bad as it looks. A touch of suspicion, a bit of jealousy. That's good for every marriage, jealousy.

JEANNE: I don't understand why he didn't throw you out long ago.

ALBERT: *(Looks admiringly at his nails)* I understand it perfectly. A funny bird, your husband.

JEANNE: *(Sits down, nervously)* I can't stand it any longer. Let's go away together. I don't care where.

ALBERT: Without money?

JEANNE: If necessary.

ALBERT: It's amazing how gullible you are. Living without money, like lovebirds in a cage, cooing and billing, that's nice, for a while. But then the glamour fades away. You begin to long for a fur coat, a nice little sports car, to go abroad for the winter; all small but understandable desires. Then you find out there's not enough money. That's not good for love. That's what makes the turtles quarrel.

JEANNE: You're right. No happiness without money.

ALBERT: Now you're talking sense. Even if you've had one too many.

JEANNE: I've had none too many.

ALBERT: *(Sniffs)* If I may believe my nose it's even more than one. I've told you often enough you must be careful. I don't want you to drink during the day. You do stupid things when you hit the bottle. That gets dangerous.

JEANNE: I haven't had a drop. Where could I get a drink here?

ALBERT: I don't know. A woman who's got the taste for booze like you have, can always find a drop somewhere.

JEANNE: Shut up. What do we have to do? I can't stand it any longer.

ALBERT: We must wait. Trust your Albert. Albert will find a way. But he's careful. He looks before he leaps. He plays the waiting game. He looks which way the cat jumps.

JEANNE: It has to happen quickly. If he gets the least shred of evidence of what is going on between us he has grounds for divorce.

ALBERT: Without a decent alimony.

JEANNE: Yes.

ALBERT: And, of course, without the benefit of the life insurance in case something unexpected happens to him.

JEANNE: Yes.

ALBERT: Don't worry. It won't happen.

JEANNE: You don't know him as well as I do. He looks soft and amiable, but I know him better.

ALBERT: I think he's rather simple.

JEANNE: Don't kid yourself.

ALBERT: I seldom do. Well, I have to go now.

JEANNE: Where to?

ALBERT: Out. Away.

JEANNE: You didn't tell me that.

ALBERT: A man has his own life. I don't have to ask your permission.

JEANNE: I don't trust you.

ALBERT: That's your problem.

JEANNE: I want you to stay with me.

ALBERT: I'll be back about six. Make something decent to eat.

JEANNE: I want to know where you're going.

ALBERT: That's none of your business. Shut up.

JEANNE: *(Blocks the door)* You've got to stay. I don't want you to go.

ALBERT: *(Astonished)* What's that? *(Growing furious)* Don't do that. Get out of the way. *(He strikes her. She falls.)*

JEANNE: If you go now you might as well stay away forever.

ALBERT: *(Grinning)* Is that so?

JEANNE: Yes. I mean it.

ALBERT: *(Goes to her and kisses her fiercely. She abandons herself completely.)* Now you see you don't mean it at all.

JEANNE: Don't keep me waiting too long.

ALBERT: That's a promise. *(At the door)* And if it makes you feel any better, I can tell you I'm going out on business. Important business. I've got a tip. A gilt-edged tip.

JEANNE: Why didn't you say so before?

ALBERT: Now you know how far you can go. Don't you?

JEANNE: Yes.

(He goes out. JEANNE, alone, picks up the poison bottle with a handkerchief and looks at it attentively.)

(The COMMERCIAL TRAVELLER enters, a pleasant-looking gentleman, immaculately dressed, with an expensive briefcase under his

arm. At first JEANNE *does not see him. He coughs. She starts.)*

JEANNE: How did you get in?

COMMERCIAL TRAVELLER: Through the door.

JEANNE: Through the door?

CT: Yes.

JEANNE: *(Amazed)* How's that possible?

CT: *(Showing key)* With the key.

JEANNE: How did you get that?

CT: I'll explain later.

JEANNE: *(Puts the bottle back)* You can't sneak into a house like that. It's against the law.

CT: If you give me only a few moments of your valuable time, I'm sure you'll understand, and probably be thankful.

JEANNE: What are you doing here?

CT: I want to talk.

JEANNE: Talk? About what?

CT: I have something to offer you.

JEANNE: I don't need anything.

CT: How do you know if you don't even know what I have to offer? I think you need it urgently.

JEANNE: I never buy anything at the door.

CT: Do I look like a man who sells at the door?

(Silence)

JEANNE: *(Hesitatingly)* No.

CT: What I have to offer is of the utmost importance to you.

JEANNE: Nonsense.

CT: Of the most pressing importance even.

JEANNE: I want you to leave.

CT: If you would only be so kind as to listen for a few moments.

JEANNE: No.

CT: Within five minutes you'll realize how interesting my offer is.

JEANNE: You must go now.

CT: In any case, let me say what I have to say.

JEANNE: I haven't got much time.

CT: One minute is all I need.

JEANNE: No. Get out of here.

CT: (*Talking now with so much earnest insistence that* JEANNE *is reluctantly becoming impressed*) I've studied you for months and months. I know almost everything about you. Perhaps more than you know yourself. That's my job. Now I'm asking you for only one minute of your time to make clear what my intentions are. One minute that can be of the greatest importance for your whole life.

(*Long silence.* JEANNE *is impressed by his words*)

JEANNE: Who are you?

CT: In a certain sense you could call me a commercial traveller.

JEANNE: I've told you already that I don't need anything.

CT: Oh, yes, you do. What I've got to sell, you need very much indeed.

JEANNE: (*Suspiciously*) And what have you got to sell?

CT: Murder.

(*Long silence*)

JEANNE: I don't understand you.

CT: I have the feeling that you understand me very well.

JEANNE: If you don't go immediately, I'll call the police.

CT: If I were you, I wouldn't do that.

JEANNE: Who are you?

CT: That doesn't matter at the moment. I could give you a name, but that would be dishonest. And in our profession honesty is the basis of success. Honesty and mutual confidence. Only when we share that can we do business.

JEANNE: Business!

CT: Yes.

JEANNE: What kind of business?

CT: That I'll explain in a few moments. You are Mrs. Jeanne Harewood, married in community of property to Ewald Harewood, Professor of Mycology, 41 years old, in good health, who has insured his life in your favor for the total of fifty thousand pounds.

JEANNE: How do you know that?

CT: Social research. Elementary. The facts are right?

JEANNE: Yes.

CT: Good. This is the most important item in your part of the agreement.

JEANNE: Agreement?

CT: Yes.

JEANNE: Who are you?

CT: I'm a broker.

JEANNE: What kind of broker?

(Silence)

CT: *(With threatening emphasis)* A death-salesman.

(Silence)

JEANNE: Go away. *(Weaker than before)*

CT: If you will be so kind as to listen for a few mom ents more, I will explain what I have to offer, though I presume you know that already.

JEANNE: I don't understand you.

CT: Actually you understand me quite well.

JEANNE: You must go.

CT: Let's stop this nonsense, Madam. We've got business to do. My time is precious and yours will be just as costly soon enough. I know everything about you and I know also that we will soon come to an understanding. Please, sit down. It makes the conversation much more pleasant. I like people to be comfortable during negotiations. (JEANNE *sits down*) You've been married for 18 years. You have a lover, Mr. Wester. He is younger than you. You're both planning to do away with your husband.

JEANNE: *(Frightened)* That's a lie.

CT: *(Sharply, irritated)* You shouldn't say that. I don't lie. I'm a skilled specialist and I know what I'm talking about.

JEANNE: How do you know what we're planning?

CT: There's a big organization behind me, Madam. A power-ful corporation. We choose our clients very carefully. A great deal of scientific research is involved, but when it's done we know our future customers better than they know themselves. You can take it from me, Madam, that you and your friend have arrived at the stage where you're playing with the thought of murder. *(Silence)* Psychologically speaking, Mrs. Harewood, you're a very inept killer. You're too emotional, which can cause fatal accidents. Mr. Wester is more careful than you are, but he lacks the refinement and analytical intelligence of the really successful expert in the life-removing industry.

JEANNE: *(Frightened)* What do you want?

CT: Fifty percent.

JEANNE: Of what?

CT: Of the proceeds.

JEANNE: Which proceeds?

CT: Everything proceeding from your husband's death. Insurance, author's rights, everything, but the most interesting item is, of course, the insurance.

JEANNE: My husband's . . . .

CT: Death. Yes. He's the only one whose death can be of advantage to both of us, and that's why I want to do business with you. I've nothing against your husband. On the contrary, during my investigations he has awakened a kind of sympathy in me. But that's beside the point. He must die.

JEANNE: But why have you come to me?

CT: It's people like you we're looking for. You don't realize how much initial research in our profession goes to waste. The average citizen doesn't know to what extent the intimate facts of his life have been laid down in the mechanical brains of the official computers. All we have to do is to combine the relevant items and to choose the most promising customers. To our mutual advantage. When we have found a future client we have, of course, to cope with all the restrictions imposed upon us by the requirements of safety, the need for sufficient profits, and the willingness of the prospective customer to cooperate. *(Silence)* Do you still want to call the police?

JEANNE: *(Breathing audibly)* No.

CT: Good. Then we can continue our negotiations. From now on you do what I say. An amateur always makes mistakes. An expert knows what he's doing. You've got that?

JEANNE: Yes.

CT: Good. It's obvious, of course, that we can't put down our agreement on paper.

JEANNE: Of course.

CT: But I'm happy to say that it has never occurred that one of our clients did not keep his promise. *(Laughs discreetly)* Imagine, Madam, what would happen if a customer would take it into his head to refuse to fulfill his part of the deal. It wouldn't turn out very well, of course. We can take care of that, I assure you. But we assume that a blunder of that order would never enter your mind.

JEANNE: Fifty percent. Isn't that a bit stiff?

CT: No. *(Silence)*

JEANNE: *(With an effort)* I thought . . . . thirty for instance.

CT: *(Smiling)* No.

JEANNE: It's an awful lot.

CT: That depends on what you get for it.

JEANNE: That's true. *(Reflectingly)* I'm curious what you have to say. I'm getting interested. *(Recovering)* That is to say, I've never had the slightest inclination to think about it. It's ridiculous. *(Goes to door)* You can go, Mr . . . eh . . . .

CT: My name doesn't matter.

JEANNE: You may go.

CT: *(Goes to her, takes her by the arm and brings her back to her chair)* Please be calm, Madam. It's all very simple. You must realize that we've already been preoccupied with this project for more than two months. I've thought of everything, and I can speak, of course, from rich experience. Without being too immodest I can say that I'm one of the foremost experts in the trade, one of the leading fieldmanagers in our world-wide corporation.

JEANNE: I've never heard of it.

CT: It's only known to the initiates. One could call our organization a multi-national. Our activities extend from the protection of small shops against criminal attacks to the thumbgreasing of even the highest officials in order to get contracts from the government for certain firms which can be called our clients. That's why we never make arrangements in writing. For a concern as big as ours that's not necessary. But let's leave that. For the moment it's important that you believe me when I say that nothing can go wrong. At least if you follow my instructions carefully. That's all you have to do.

JEANNE: *(As from a dream)* You're crazy.

CT: I'm a businessman.

JEANNE: I won't do it.

CT: That's how most people react. You resist, you won't have anything to do with me, but I shall carefully explain what you have to do, you will listen, and then you will carry out what I have told you to do. Very carefully, of course, for your life depends on it. I hope you'll excuse me for not paying much attention to your objections. We haven't much time. Your husband will soon be here. Sit down, please. *(JEANNE does so)*

JEANNE: I'm so nervous all of a sudden.

CT: *(Sharply)* It's of the utmost importance that you keep your nerves under control, Madam.

JEANNE: Just one small drop. It makes me feel better. A little drop is enough.

CT: I don't think this is the appropriate time for a little drop, as you like to call it. When everything is over you can have a drink. But not now. Or perhaps you want to give up our plan? Hesitation is often very dangerous. *(Silence)*

JEANNE: Go on.

CT: All right, we'll go on. First the facts. Your husband will arrive presently, accompanied by his assistant.

JEANNE: Oh, that piece of baggage.

CT: You don't like her?

JEANNE: No. Too prim for her age.

CT: I think it's a useful coincidence that you don't like her, for a part of our plan is that she'll join your husband in entering eternity. I'm sorry about that, because she's innocent. I mean she isn't worth a penny as a corpse, but I see no other solution. I presume you have no objections to her going with him?

JEANNE: No.

CT: Good. They will arrive soon with a nice load of mushrooms they have gathered this afternoon, a kind called Boletus Mirabellus. It's their intention to make a nice little snack of it. They often do that at the laboratory. Today is the first time they've found enough courage to have a meal of mushrooms here together.

JEANNE: How do you know that?

CT: That's my job. A matter of research. You know the B.M.?

JEANNE: No. I don't know anything about mushrooms.

CT: A succulent, spicy edible mushroom with an aftertaste of nuts. (*Takes a book from the bookcase, looks up something*) Look. The color is a bit muddy, but it's quite tasty. (*Puts the book back*) Of course, one has to be an expert for the B.M. Otherwise accidents might happen. You have to know that there is another mushroom which has the disagreeable habit of growing next to the B.M. and which looks very much like it. It is called, very appropriately, Boletus Pseudomirabellus, and is extremely poisonous. (*Takes a little bottle from his briefcase, gives it to* JEANNE) Incidentally, your husband is one of the greatest, if not the only, expert on this disagreeable kind of mushroom. He has written a very deep-probing paper on it which has aroused the most enthusiastic admiration in mycological circles. (*Goes to the shelf*) This, Madam, is an extract of this poisonous fungus, the Boletus Pseudomirabellus. (*Puts it back; silence*)

JEANNE: What am I supposed to do?

CT: You must only put a few drops, not more than three, in the pan in which the harmless Mirabellus soon will simmer. After their meal the professor and his companion won't be able to blow a feather. They will be dead. An accident. One Pseudomirabellus has got into the meal. A very regrettable accident. That's all. Not more than three drops; otherwise the taste of the meal might be affected, which might cause them to be suspicious. Not more than three drops and it will net you fifty thousand pounds, tax-free.

JEANNE: One half of it.

CT: You're right, but still . . . .

JEANNE: *(Reflectingly)* Yes, it's a lot of money, indeed.

CT: Death is good business.

JEANNE: It's ridiculous. The whole thing.

CT: It's very logical.

JEANNE: You seem to forget that a man like my husband would never pick the wrong mushroom. The police will surely think of that.

CT: Every man can make a mistake once in his life.

JEANNE: But he would never make that kind of mistake. I know him.

CT: The facts, Madam, won't leave room for any other interpretation. I've done extensive research on my plan and I'm sure nothing can go wrong.

JEANNE: Who guarantees that?

CT: I do.

JEANNE: I don't know you.

CT: You will get to know me. My plan is simple, well-constructed, without flaws or risks.

JEANNE: *(Reflectingly)* All right. There's something in what you say.

CT: And now we must hurry. First a rehearsal. We can't leave anything to chance. *(To* JEANNE*)* I'm your husband now. *(He assumes the role)* I'm standing over there near the gas ring. I'm putting a pinch of salt, some slices of onion and a drop of wine into the mushrooms. I'm sniffing voluptuously. I nod to my assistant. In a little while we'll have a real feast, for the first time in my own study. Then you enter. You disturb their intimacy. You say: Someone on the line for you, Ewald.

(During this rehearsal ALBERT *can be seen through the french windows, coming from the garden. He sets them slightly ajar.)*

JEANNE: *(Goes out and returns immediately)* Someone on the line for you, Ewald.

CT: I'm busy now. Tell him to ring again in an hour.

JEANNE: And then?

CT: It's Eriksen.

JEANNE: It's Eriksen. *(Halts)* How can you know that?

CT: What?

JEANNE: That Eriksen will ring.

CT: *(Firmly)* Eriksen will ring.

JEANNE: It's Eriksen. He says it's urgent.

CT: Eriksen? That's important. I can't let him wait. *(To his imaginary assistant)* I'll be back soon, Helen. *(Goes to the door)* The Professor is gone now. It will be arranged that he's occupied for at least five minutes.

JEANNE: How?

CT: You can best leave these details to me.

JEANNE: And then?

CT: After some minutes you enter again and tell Helen that your husband wants her assistance. That's a fact. She has notes your husband needs in his conversation. You then go to the kitchen. This room is now empty. The Mirabellus on the gas ring is simmering with an appetizing fragrance. Now everything must happen as quickly as possible. *(Demonstrating)* You enter again through the garden door— *(He turns, pointing at the door and* ALBERT *hastily withdraws)* —and put three drops of the poison in the pan. After you've done that, you disappear through the garden. When he has finished his telephone conversation the Professor and his assistant will come back to start their meal. An hour or so later you come to call your husband to dinner. He will not be able to partake of it. He will be dead and the same goes for his assistant. I'm sorry for her, but that's the way it has to be. Business before pity. Is that clear?

JEANNE: Yes.

CT: Will you repeat it, please?

JEANNE: Telephone. Eriksen. Call Helen. Together with her to the telephone. Then to the kitchen. The room is empty. I enter again through the garden door. Three drops in the pan. Back through the garden.

CT: All right. *(Bows)* I wish you luck. Money softens the pangs of crime. You'll see me again, for the final settlement. Fifty percent. *(Looks at watch)* Your husband can arrive any moment now. I must go. No, it's not necessary to see me out. *(He turns, turns again, and looks reflectively at* JEANNE*)* Don't worry. I've invested three months of research in this project. Three months of work and a life full of experience. I know you, I know your lover, I know your husband and I know that poor girl who presently has to die innocently; and when I claim that I know these people I mean that I really know them. The poison in this bottle is infallible. Nothing can go wrong. Up to now my projects have never failed.

JEANNE: *(Hesitatingly)* Well, I must say it sounds like a damn good plan.

CT: Thank you, Madam. A craftsman in our profession sometimes appreciates words of praise. We get them so seldom, due to the peculiar circumstances in which we have to operate.

(ALBERT *enters*)

ALBERT: *(Coughs)* May I ask you, sir, what you're doing here?

JEANNE: Albert!

ALBERT: The same as always. And who might this gentleman be?

CT: My name doesn't matter.

ALBERT: Will you be so kind as to make yourself scarce, sir?

CT: You're Mr. Albert Wester, I presume?

ALBERT: Yes. You know me?

CT: I know you quite well.

ALBERT: *(Suspiciously)* Is that so? How well?

CT: In my estimation you're worth ten years of solitary confinement. At least with the proofs I have at my disposal.

ALBERT: *(Menacingly)* You dirty bastard, I'll . . . .

CT: One moment, please Mr. Wester. We're both in the same profession, though in different branches. In a certain sense we could call each other colleagues, and it's better for colleagues to talk than to fight. *(Reads from a piece of paper)* You met Professor Harewood last summer when he was with his wife *(Bows to* JEANNE*)* in Cannes. The Professor took an immediate liking to you and invited you to his home.

ALBERT: *(Musingly)* You do know a lot, don't you?

CT: That's my profession, sir. Knowledge is half the results. You make your living by blackmail and sometimes by less tasteful activities, but let's leave that for the moment.

JEANNE: *(Artificially cheerful)* I think it's now time for a little bracer.

ALBERT: *(Shakes her)* Keep your silly brains together.

CT: This gentleman is right, Madam. You must keep your head clear.

ALBERT: Go on.

CT: Madam and I have just been discussing the most appropriate means of doing away with her husband and your friend, Professor Harewood, which incidentally has been on your minds for some time.

ALBERT: Are you mad?

CT: No, I'm a businessman with a perfectly sound proposition.

ALBERT: *(Reflectingly)* I see. A project.

CT: You might call it that.

ALBERT: I don't like the idea.

CT: From what I know of you, it can't be on moral grounds.

ALBERT: The Professor has been a good friend to me. I've learned to like him during the past few months.

CT: Those feelings do you credit, but, of course, they must not hinder you in the execution of what has to be done.

ALBERT: Of course not. By the way, would a small advance be possible?

CT: No, Mr. Wester, we never participate in the financing of our projects.

ALBERT: Pity. I happen to need a little loose change. Some debts I've run up in the last few days. But never mind. I still have a little scheme left for emergencies. What's in it for me?

CT: As a close collaborator of Mrs. Harewood you must come to an agreement with her in the first place. If you allow me to make an estimate from experience, however, I think that your part, after deduction of death duties and other taxes, will come to close to ten thousand pounds.

ALBERT: *(Impressed, whistles)* Ten thousand quid?

CT: The usual bonus for a close collaborator. *(Looks at his watch)* But I have to go now. Your husband will be here shortly. You know what you have to do. It's simple, efficient and infallible. *(Goes to the door, turns)* Madam, I'd like to give you a little advice. Don't start playing with the thought that murder, executed as a hobby, could have the slightest chance of success. It can only have the most damaging consequences. You wouldn't think of trying to repair your own TV set, and yet you're contemplating attempting a layman's homicide. I assure you, Madam, that a good murder is a lot more difficult than replacing a TV tube. And that goes for you, too, sir. I'll see you again soon, when everything is over. *(Bows, exits)*

ALBERT: *(After a long silence)* So he had a plan?

JEANNE: Yes.

ALBERT: With poison?

JEANNE: Yes.

ALBERT: The damned amateur. How much did he want?

JEANNE: Fifty percent.

ALBERT: Is he crazy?

JEANNE: *(Musingly)* He talked so convincingly.

ALBERT: They all do. I know them. They pounce upon the suckers of the world and ask fifty percent. Mostly they get their way, but not with Albert. Albert is too smart for them. *(Thinks)* He wanted to poison the fine meal of fungi dear Ewald and his little dove are going to guzzle? A sound idea in itself. After all, he's dug up the fact that the professor is going to dine for the first time with his secretary in his own home. A nice piece of work. Let's say, worth twenty percent; and not a penny more. But what an ass-headed idiot this man must be to think that poison from a bottle would do the trick. I've told you already how dangerous that is.

JEANNE: Yes, that's true. But when he explained it to me it sounded convincing.

ALBERT: I've got something far better. *(Gets a large envelope from his briefcase, takes a very big and very yellow mushroom from it)*

JEANNE: What's that?

ALBERT: This is the real stuff. A genuine Boleto Pseudo-mirabellus. *(Goes to the bookcase, takes a book and leafs through it)* Look. This is a real Boletus Mirabellus and this is the Boletus Pseudomirabellus. They're nearly alike, but if you eat them the result is quite different.

JEANNE: How do you know?

ALBERT: You think that I'm nothing more than mother's original nitwit, because I don't talk with a potato in my throat, but I'm not as dumb as you think I am.

JEANNE: It's the same mushroom that man mentioned.

ALBERT: Quite simple. Professional snooping teaches you a lot. I found this nasty piece of toadstool in your husband's bedroom. A straying bird, you know, picks up a grain or two.

JEANNE: Won't he miss it?

ALBERT: No, it was carefully hidden in one of the drawers, where he keeps some of his equipment.

JEANNE: Yes, he often works in his bedroom when he can't sleep, but he'll know the difference at a glance.

ALBERT: Not in a nice stew, and—besides—he won't have time.

JEANNE: That's true.

ALBERT: So now it's simply a matter of a real mistake. Now there's no chance that a nosy policeman will notice there's been poison in the stew. No, dear, it's now the genuine article. We don't need that blown-up gentleman with his ridiculous propositions. We run this business on our own.

JEANNE:He warned us especially against that.

ALBERT: Of course.

JEANNE: He can put the police on the trail by telling them that the meal has been poisoned.

ALBERT: *(Even more enthusiastic)* But it hasn't, darling. That's what the bloke couldn't know. It's now the real Pseudomirabellus. There's no risk at all. Everybody makes a mistake once in his life. Your husband has done that. With fatal consequences.

JEANNE: Are you quite sure it's the real Pseudo?

ALBERT: Quite. Your husband has a very clear way of explaining things. His notes and the picture in this handbook leave no doubt. There was even a label attached to this beauty.

JEANNE: Won't he miss it?

ALBERT: He won't have time. And, besides, I've put the label on another piece of the stuff.

JEANNE: So what are we going to do now?

ALBERT: Leave everything to me. The only thing you have to do is follow this fellow's instructions about luring Ewald away with the story of Eriksen on the phone. I must say, that's a fine piece of work.

JEANNE: What do you know about Eriksen?

ALBERT: I read his correspondence with Ewald. It's about the typography of an article. I know a lot about that. At one time printing was my business. Fine printing, one could say. *(The sound of an engine is heard)*

JEANNE: There he is.

ALBERT: Don't be afraid. *(Kisses* JEANNE *perfunctorily)* It's better that Ewald doesn't see me now. *(Looks at watch)* Yes, I still have some time left. I've got something important to do. See you soon. *(Exits)*

*(*JEANNE *is alone. She remains motionless, reflecting on all that has happened. Then she goes to the bookcase, takes the bottle of whisky and the glass, prepares herself for a drink, hears noises from outside,*

and hastily puts bottle and glass back. EWALD *and* HELEN *enter.
They fit exactly the description by the* CT. *He is about forty, mild-
mannered, absent-minded, scholarly; she may be thirty, is dressed in
a plain sweater, wears spectacles, is simple and devoted. There is a
marked silence when they see* JEANNE.*)*

EWALD: Good afternoon, Jeanne.

JEANNE: Good afternoon.

HELEN: Good afternoon, Mrs. Harewood.

JEANNE: I was looking for a box of matches. I had none left
in the kitchen.

EWALD: *(Takes a box near the gas ring, gives it to her)* Here you are.

HELEN: What shall I do with the Mirabellus, Professor?

EWALD: You can put them here, Helen.

HELEN: *(After a long, disagreeable silence)* Well, I think I'll go
now. *(Looks in her book)* You know that tomorrow at ten o'clock
you have an appointment with Henderson of the Tropical
Institute?

EWALD: Oh, yes, that's right. I nearly forgot it. Perhaps you
can stay for a few moments. I need your help. You think you
can manage?

HELEN: Of course, Professor.

EWALD: *(To* JEANNE*)* We have a spot of work to do, you know.

JEANNE: Shall I make dinner for you?

EWALD: Dinner? Oh no. We have found a lot of Mirabellus
and I think that will be more than a meal in itself. *(To* HELEN*)*
Of course you're going to stay to help me finish them off.
(Silence) You found even more than I did.

HELEN: I don't know. I have . . . eh . . . something to do.

EWALD: Nonsense.

JEANNE: You can stay if you like.

EWALD: I think we have all we need. Onions, paprika. Yes, everything.

JEANNE: I think I'll leave you alone, then.

EWALD: Very well.

JEANNE: I hope you enjoy your meal.

EWALD: *(To* HELEN*)* And you too, Miss Engels.

HELEN: Thank you very much, Mrs. Harewood.

(Exit JEANNE*)*

HELEN: You shouldn't have invited me, Professor. The whole situation is horrible.

EWALD: Professor?

HELEN: I'm not yet used to calling you by your Christian name.

EWALD: You'll get used to it soon enough.

HELEN: At the lab everything is so much easier. When we are working together, it's natural. But here I feel a stranger.

EWALD: That's not necessary. You are in my home.

HELEN: It's also her home.

EWALD: This is my room, my place. She has no business here. I've got my books, my test tubes, my microscopes, my gas ring. Here is where you belong, too.

HELEN: *(Walking around)* Yes, that's how I feel. It's nice here. *(Sniffs)* I smell that filthy pipe of yours.

EWALD: *(Lights the pipe)* Let's unpack the loot.

HELEN: I haven't got any appetite.

EWALD: You will . . . Mirabellus with a bit of onion, paprika, a teeny whiff of garlic and a pinch of thyme will give you a nice appetite.

HELEN: I could kill her.

EWALD: *(Starts)* What's that?

HELEN: Her. She's ruining your life.

EWALD: You can't say that.

HELEN: Why not? It's true. I hate her. The way she destroys you and still hangs on to you, like a parasite.

EWALD: *(Suddenly, very fiercely, without his good humor)* I forbid you to say that again, do you hear me?

HELEN: *(Frightened)* It was just an impulse.

EWALD: It can be dangerous. Wishes have power. Imagine Jeanne having an accident and getting killed.

HELEN: But she won't have an accident. Not somebody like Jeanne. Fathers with a lot of children, they have accidents, but not somebody like her.

EWALD: You never know. Hate is poisonous. Some people die from hate.

HELEN: I didn't know you were so superstitious.

EWALD: You must promise never to say it again.

HELEN: I'm sorry. You're too kind.

EWALD: I can't be different from what I am.

HELEN: You shouldn't be different.

EWALD: I've many faults and bad traits.

HELEN: They belong to you.

EWALD: I've got more of them than you think.

HELEN: I can't imagine.

EWALD: Let's begin.

HELEN: *(Takes a bunch of mushrooms out of her bag)* They look good.

EWALD: Yes. Very good. *(Looks at them)* Imagine what would happen if we should cook a Pseudomirabellus with the rest, by accident.

HELEN: *(Laughs)* It would cost you your job. It would be proof of gross ignorance.

EWALD: It would be too late to mind then, but don't worry, they all look good. You know, when I was a student I happened to swallow a mouthful of a stew with one non-edible fungus in it. *(Silence)* Since that time I always check them carefully before I put the mushrooms into the pan.

HELEN: I trust you unconditionally. I'll down anything you put in front of me.

EWALD: And I promise not to disappoint you. They must be cleaned.

HELEN: That's my work.

EWALD: No, I'll do it. You are my guest.

HELEN: I was under the impression that we still had some work to do. That's the pretext you used to lure me to your home.

EWALD: As far as the meal is concerned you're my guest and therefore I'll take care of that. But if you want something to do, why don't you fill two glasses with wine? *(He prepares the mushrooms, his back to her and to the public)*

HELEN: I see no glasses and no wine.

EWALD: In my briefcase.

HELEN: You've thought of everything. That's not like you.

EWALD: It's a special occasion.

HELEN: *(With the glasses)* To our work.

EWALD: *(Solemnly)* To our future.

HELEN: *(Suddenly bursting out)* Why did you marry her?

EWALD: We were both young. My father was a rich man.

HELEN: Rich? I didn't know that.

EWALD: He lived like a rich man. On quicksand. People like that can live like that. I would never be able to survive if I always had to look for the next stepping-stone. When my father died everything had to be sold. I was already married. Jeanne has never forgiven me for not preventing the catastrophe. In the beginning she thought that I would take over the business and make it prosper again.

HELEN: Of course you were not the man for it.

EWALD: I could very well have been the man for it. My father was an amiable braggart who could squeeze money from the most suspicious banker. I had far more brains than he did. I could have easily brought new life into the business and made a success of it. Of course I didn't do that.

HELEN: Why not? *(Pours again, they drink)*

EWALD: Because any man in his right senses can see how ridiculous it is to earn more money than you need to be reasonably happy. I despise the kind of business people I would have to deal with. I like doing research work; patiently looking for clues and collaborating with associates in the same field in a small laboratory. I want to achieve something in that tiny part of science I can really master. I don't think I have done too badly.

HELEN: You've done magnificently.

EWALD: I'm not very happy, but I'm as happy as a man can be in my work. I've always known that beyond a certain limit money is useless. Of course, I never managed to make that clear to Jeanne.

HELEN: And then she started to drink?

EWALD: Oh, no, she always drank, but I never suspected it. I was very green, you know. I'm still rather naive, but now I know that I am.

HELEN: Why don't you get a divorce?

EWALD: It's impossible.

HELEN: Why?

EWALD: She wants too much. I can't afford it. *(Silence)*

HELEN: I don't want to talk about it any more.

EWALD: Neither do I. Let's take care of the Mirabellus. *(Washing the mushrooms)* A very tasty fungus, but you must know that the underside is a bit bitter and must be cut off. Can you fill the glasses again?

HELEN: *(Filling)* We mustn't get soused.

EWALD: Don't worry. You've been temperate up till now. A drop of wine whets the appetite. I'll bet you feel more hungry now.

HELEN: That's true.

EWALD: Now the mushrooms go into the pan. *(Puts them in)* They have to cook in their own juice. Some onion, then the herbs. It's very simple. They'll be ready in about fifteen minutes. Will you set the table?

HELEN: Where, for heaven's sake? In this mess?

EWALD: Put the books on the floor. You'll find everything in the cupboard here. *(Looks to her activities)* I like seeing you setting the table.

HELEN: *(Tonelessly)* Yes.

EWALD: I think we should do this more often.

(While HELEN is preparing the table, EWALD goes behind her and makes a movement as if to embrace her. She feels it and turns expectantly, but he turns back. HELEN continues her work. The door opens and ALBERT enters. HELEN and EWALD jump.)

ALBERT: I'm not disturbing you, I hope. *(Silence. ALBERT moves into the room)* Of course not. A good friend never disturbs. *(To HELEN)* I don't think we've met. *(HELEN starts and turns her back)*

EWALD: *(Forcing himself to accept the situation)* This is Albert Wester, a . . . eh . . . a friend. Miss Engels, my assistant.

ALBERT: *(Looks at her impudently)* Assistant. *(To EWALD)* Yes, Jeanne told me that you had an assistant.

EWALD: What are you doing here?

ALBERT: Oh, I just came to have a little talk with you. Ah, the bottle is already on the table. That's nice of you. Thank you. I will. *(Fills a glass)* A good year. A drop of wine is good for friendship, I always say.

EWALD: Why did you come?

ALBERT: I told you already. To talk with you.

EWALD: Another time would suit me better. You see I'm busy.

ALBERT: No. I'm sorry. Another time would be too late.

(Long silence. EWALD forces himself to remain calm. HELEN looks petrified)

EWALD: What have you got to tell me?

ALBERT: Oh, a couple of things. I should say a little talk between two friends. Privately. *(Silence)*

HELEN: Eh . . . I . . . I'll be back soon.

EWALD: *(To ALBERT)* I'll give you ten minutes. No more.

(Exit HELEN)

ALBERT: Ten minutes should be enough.

EWALD: What do you want?

ALBERT: I need money.

EWALD: What? I paid you only yesterday.

ALBERT: Yes, I know, but some unexpected debts popped up. Rather urgent I must say. You know how it is, you think you've still got something left, and then it appears that the old wallet

is empty. Then you remember that you still have a very good
friend who was always willing to help you when you were in
need. What does Albert think then? Albert thinks: I'll pay a
visit to that dear friend. *(Silence)*

EWALD: *(With restraint)* How much?

ALBERT: Oh, I think five hundred would go quite a long way.

EWALD: What?

ALBERT: Was my pronunciation not clear enough? That's
because of the wine. Wine blurs the words. But I'm quite
willing to repeat it. Five hundred pounds. Five—hundred—
pounds—sterling.

EWALD: Impossible.

ALBERT: What a pity. What an awful pity.

EWALD: I gave you two hundred yesterday. You know I'm not
rich. I had to borrow it. And you promised it would be the
last payment. Now five hundred again. Impossible.

ALBERT: Yet you have to cough it up.

EWALD: How?

ALBERT: That's your problem. Not mine.
to repeat it. Five hundred pounds. Five—hundred—pounds—
sterling.

EWALD: Impossible.

ALBERT: What a pity. What an awful pity.

EWALD: I gave you two hundred yesterday. You know I'm not
rich. I had to borrow it. And you promised it would be the
last payment. Now five hundred again. Impossible.

ALBERT: Yet you have to cough it up.

EWALD: How?

ALBERT: That's your problem. Not mine.

EWALD: And yesterday you promised it would be the last time.

ALBERT: Did I really say that?

EWALD: *(Tiredly)* Yes.

ALBERT: You must've made a mistake.

EWALD: No, I didn't.

ALBERT: You move me. You're one of those people whom people like me always dream of meeting. One of those soft, simple, unimpeachable human beings who have only once made a mis-step. People like you think that words mean what they mean. If I wasn't so hard pressed I'd let you keep the money. I would just make you a present of it.

EWALD: My God. No! I won't give it to you.

ALBERT: Oh, how annoying that would be.

EWALD: *(Enraged)* I could kill you.

ALBERT: Who could've thought that so much blood-lust could exist in such a soft man?

EWALD: If he is sufficiently provoked. *(Breathes deeply)* I've made up my mind.

ALBERT: You're a brave fellow.

EWALD: I can't go on like this.

ALBERT: You know what I have in my possession.

EWALD: Yes.

ALBERT: By the way, I've never understood why you left the proof of your mis-step . . . for in my opinion it's only a little mis-step . . . just like that in your desk drawers, where anyone the least bit curious could find it.

EWALD: I could never imagine that a man who came into my house as a friend would search my desk.

ALBERT: Let this be a good lesson to you. Don't trust anybody. Ever. No man is to be trusted. That's what I learned early in my life, and it has done me a lot of good. Of course, you've had bad luck. You couldn't have know that it's my job to rummage in the desks of people who have learned to trust me. I'm a nice guy and people trust me rather quickly. Only after a while do they find out that it costs them money. I make a living from the confidence of my fellow men. *(Threateningly)* And if you don't pay, Ewald, the world will know that your work on the Harabolet, which is so highly praised in scientific circles, was stolen from your late colleague Derksen, and that I have in my possession the original manuscript as a proof of your plagiarism. No, Ewald, that was not nice, to publish another man's scientific study under your own name. It's simply stealing!

EWALD: Stop it.

ALBERT: In God's name how did you ever get the silly idea? I don't understand that. I'm quite a good judge of character and I have always seen you as an honest, simple mushroom freak. And then such a thing pops up. Really, Ewald, you ought to be ashamed.

EWALD: *(More to himself than to* ALBERT*)* For years I had been working on the subject. I had discovered the development and metamorphosis of the Harabolet. It had always been one of the secrets of mycology. And then I found that Derksen was working along the same lines. He had made even more progress than I. It was a horrible shock. I was already sure to be old Melcher's successor. He had the chair and would retire soon. Derksen let me read his manuscript. I knew that all my work had become useless. Then he died unexpectedly. He had a weak heart. Everybody knew that. He lived in retirement. Only his old housekeeper took care of him. Nobody knew about the manuscript. Till this day I don't understand why I did it, but when things had gone so far I couldn't go back. I've been an awful coward, but I had the justification that I had discovered on my own strength what Derksen had found, too, though I must admit he had advanced further. When he died I somehow had the feeling that I had made his investigations myself. Of course, I should have made a confession at that time, but I lacked the courage. *(Silence)* I will have to retire.

ALBERT: That's rather hasty, isn't it? We can talk about it. I've asked five hundred.

EWALD: I don't have it.

ALBERT: Ah, ah, never tell lies, Ewald. Honesty is the best policy. You should know that by now. You have four hundred in your moneybox. The last installment on your mortgage.

EWALD: *(Bitter)* Why didn't you pinch the money?

ALBERT: *(Indignantly)* I'm no petty thief.

EWALD: It's all I have.

ALBERT: All right. Then you'll get your manuscript for four hundred. I'm not as hard as I look.

EWALD: I don't trust you.

ALBERT: Nice people don't say those things.

EWALD: I know your kind. What assurance can you give me that you won't plague me again?

ALBERT: I'll give you your manuscript.

EWALD: You could've made God knows how many copies.

ALBERT: My word of honor. *(Silence)* And if that doesn't suit you, you can have it as you want. If I don't get that four hundred I'll have you in the pillory tomorrow.

EWALD: This *must* be the last time.

ALBERT: That's a promise.

EWALD: You said that yesterday, too.

ALBERT: But now you have my word of honor. And the manuscript.

EWALD: *(Taking the money from the box)* Here's the money. Where's the manuscript?

ALBERT: Here it is. *(They exchange. He counts the money, superfluously)* In small bills. Just as I like it. I don't even count them. That proves how I trust you.

EWALD: If you bother me again . . . or if it comes out that you have had a copy made . . . .

ALBERT: Then what?

EWALD: Then that will be the end. Listen carefully. *(In deep earnest)* I mean it. This must be the last time. Either I'll resign as Professor . . .

ALBERT: Nobody will be the better for that.

EWALD: Or I'll kill you.

(Long silence)

ALBERT: I like you, Ewald, really, and that's why I promise you that this is the last time. Really.

(EWALD goes to the bookcase and gets the bottle of whisky and a glass from behind the books. He fills it and takes a gulp)

EWALD: I hope you realize how sincerely I meant that.

ALBERT: That's all right. But wouldn't it be polite to offer a touch of the stuff to an old friend? After all we've just done a bit of business.

(EWALD looks at him, astonished, then shrugs his shoulders. He goes to his cooking corner, takes a glass which he first carefully wipes, and then puts it on a tray. He fills this glass with whisky and offers it, still on the tray, to ALBERT)

ALBERT: *(Drinking)* Your health.

(EWALD puts his own glass on the tray and takes both glasses to his cooking corner where he washes them but not very carefully. One glass he carefully polishes with a cloth and puts it back, together with the bottle, behind the books. It must be clearly visible that he keeps the cloth in his hands while doing this.)

ALBERT: Good stuff, that. Why do you keep it there?

EWALD: I can't concentrate on my work as well as I used to, and a drop now and then helps, especially when I have to work at night. I don't want JEANNE to know it. It would be a bad example for her.

ALBERT: That's true. She does the daftest things when she's under the influence. It's good that she doesn't know she can get it here.

EWALD: Nobody would look for a bottle of bonded whisky behind the Collected Works of Pope. Pope is a boring poet. These books are left from my schooldays. A yard of unreadable metrical feet makes a good hiding place.

ALBERT: *(Going to bookcase)* You're right. No one would look for a snort behind Pope.

(EWALD *goes to the gas ring and stirs the contents of the pan. He tastes it.)*

ALBERT: What's that?

EWALD: Boletus Mirabellus. A fungus.

ALBERT: What are you doing?

EWALD: Cooking the stuff. It's very tasty when properly prepared, but only when it's freshly picked. Do you want a taste?

ALBERT: No, thank you, it might be poisonous.

EWALD: It's my specialty to see that it's not poisonous.

ALBERT: Every specialist makes mistakes.

(HELEN *enters and remains hesitantly in the doorway.)*

EWALD: Come in.

ALBERT: Well, I've got to toddle off. Everything's okay now. *(Exits)*

HELEN: What's happened?

EWALD: I can't tell you yet.

HELEN: Sorry I asked.

EWALD: No. I think you've a right to know. But it must wait.

HELEN: I only wanted to help. It wasn't curiosity.

EWALD: I know. *(Goes to the gas ring)* The Mirabellus will soon be ready. I don't want our meal to be disturbed.

HELEN: All right. I'll be as cheerful as they come. *(She begins to prepare the table. The telephone lamp lights up.)* The telephone.

EWALD: I don't want to be disturbed. Jeanne will answer.

(JEANNE enters.)

JEANNE: It's cosy in here. *(Silence)* That smells good. *(Goes to the gas ring)* Is it ready?

EWALD: Only a few minutes.

JEANNE: Pity I don't like mushrooms.

EWALD: You can always try.

JEANNE: No, it's too late for that. There's someone on the line for you.

EWALD: Tell him I'm not here.

JEANNE: I told him that, but he told me to tell you, you had to be here. He had a nice voice.

EWALD: Who was it?

JEANNE: Eriksen.

HELEN: Eriksen? Already? He must have worked hard.

EWALD: I'm coming. *(Goes. HELEN continues the preparations for the meal)*

JEANNE: I hope you enjoy your meal. *(Goes)*

(HELEN *is alone. She is very sad. She sits down at the table and weeps a little. Then she tries to restore her face with powder and lipstick.* JEANNE *enters again and looks mockingly at her.* HELEN *sees her, starts, feels ashamed, then rises.*)

JEANNE: My husband is asking for you.

HELEN: I'll get my notes.

(*She looks in her pocketbook, gets nervous under* JEANNE'*s stare, then finds what she needs and goes.* JEANNE *goes with her. The stage remains empty for a few moments. The little pot is steaming. Then* ALBERT *comes in through the garden door. He throws the poisonous mushroom into the pan and goes away quickly. The stage is empty again. The audience must be aware of the fact that the steaming pan contains poison now.* HELEN *enters. She continues the restoration of her face. When she is ready and has put on her rather old-fashioned spectacles again, she turns her attention to the simmering mushrooms, throws some herbs in the pot, etc.* EWALD *enters. He, too, goes to the pot and inspects the contents*)

HELEN: What are you doing?

EWALD: Looking to see if they are done all right.

HELEN: Oh yes, to a turn. That phone call lasted an eternity.

EWALD: I've never heard Eriksen jaw so much.

HELEN: He's getting older.

EWALD: Yes, I think so.

HELEN: When will he publish the article?

EWALD: Perhaps next month. He shouldn't have yakked so much about those printing details. The article is good, and that's what counts. Not the printing.

HELEN: It's one of the best you ever wrote. It's not like Eriksen to make such a fuss about those things.

EWALD: No. Funny.

HELEN: And I don't know why he had to ring you up.

EWALD: Everything he asked he should've known. Oh well, he was drowned in a cold. I suppose that was why. His voice sounded like a rasp. The things he proposed are really quite unimportant.

HELEN: Even I could put them in.

EWALD: As a matter of fact I've thought about that.

HELEN: And now we'll have our meal.

(HELEN *puts the mushrooms on the plates.* EWALD *fills the glasses with wine, his back to the audience so that nobody can see how he manipulates the glasses. He turns, with two full glasses in his hands, and gives one to* HELEN. *They sit down, raise their glasses and start to eat.*)

EWALD: It's nice here with you.

HELEN: Funny, isn't it?

EWALD: What?

HELEN: It's the first time we are eating Boletus together.

EWALD: Let's hope it won't be the last time.

(*They raise their glasses again and go on eating. The curtain falls only when it is clear that they have already swallowed a large helping of the mushrooms.*)

[END OF ACT I]

Act Two

(The stage is empty. The table is still laid for the Boletus meal, but it is clear that a lot of it has been eaten.

JEANNE *enters. She starts when she sees that there is not a living—or dead—soul in the room. She looks around. She sniffs at the pot of mushrooms, then she hears voices from the garden.*

EWALD *and* HELEN *enter.* JEANNE *is hardly able to suppress a cry)*

EWALD: What's the matter?

JEANNE: I don't know. I was just . . . startled.

EWALD: Why?

JEANNE: I don't know. Perhaps because you came in so suddenly.

EWALD: We only went for a walk in the garden. A bit of fresh air after the meal.

JEANNE: *(Recovering)* I . . . I thought . . . that you would have gone already.

EWALD: No, we haven't gone yet. *(Silence)* Though we intend to go, when we've cleared up the mess here.

JEANNE: Did you . . . did you eat the mushrooms?

EWALD: Oh yes, they were quite good.

JEANNE: Will you be long?

EWALD: First I'll see Helen home, and then I have quite a lot to do at the lab.

JEANNE: Then you'll lock up?

EWALD: Yes. You can go to bed when you like.

JEANNE: Fine. *(Starts to go)*

EWALD: By the way, I'll have to work when I come back. My lectures for Tuesday aren't ready yet. Perhaps you would put some coffee in the thermos?

JEANNE: Of course.

EWALD: Thank you. *(Silence)*

JEANNE: I'll go now. *(Exits)*

EWALD: We'll have to go, too.

HELEN: *(A little depressed)* Very well.

EWALD: What's the matter, darling? Don't you feel well?

HELEN: Oh yes. I feel all right. As a matter of fact I'm quite happy.

EWALD: There was a tinge of sadness in your voice.

HELEN: Perhaps because I feel so happy. I'm all dizzy.

EWALD: That's because of the wine. We shouldn't have drunk so much.

HELEN: Oh yes, it was delicious. Everything was perfect. Picking the Boletus, our meal together, the wine.

EWALD: And that's why you're a bit sad, too?

HELEN: Yes, that's why. *(Silence)* Because it will soon be over.

EWALD: *(Empties the bottle into the two glasses)* Therefore we must enjoy it as long as it lasts. Your health.

HELEN: I'm really getting drunk.

EWALD: Nonsense.

HELEN: The world is turning.

EWALD: To which side?

Helen: *(Reflecting)* To the left.

Ewald: That's good. Now you must empty this glass. Then the world will turn to the right, which will neutralize the movement.

(They drink.)

Helen: I've never seen you so happy. I'm glad. You were so melancholy lately that I began to worry.

Ewald: We have never polished off a whole bottle of Lafitte '72 together.

Helen: Lafitte '72?

Ewald: Yes. An extremely good year. Sunny and cold. that's what a Lafitte needs. This was my last bottle.

Helen: The more I know you, the stranger you are to me. I know you're an expert where mushrooms are concerned, but I didn't know you were a judge of wines. To me they are all red and a bit sour and delicious and they make me dizzy.

Ewald: *(Suddenly concerned)* Sit down. Are you sure there's nothing wrong?

Helen: Only a little bit dizzy from the wine.

Ewald: Let me feel your pulse.

Helen: It's not as bad as all that. I'm not ill. But it's just that I don't drink very often.

Ewald: *(Sharply)* Let me feel your pulse. *(Does so)* A bit fast.

Helen: That's because you're holding my hand.

Ewald: Try to say what you really feel.

Helen: I cannot and I don't intend to.

Ewald: I must know.

Helen: It's gone already. Pity.

Ewald: So you don't feel pain?

HELEN: No. Not at all.

EWALD: *(With relief)* So you're only a little bit tipsy.

HELEN: That's what I tried to tell you all the time.

EWALD: Don't you feel ashamed?

HELEN: No, because it's your fault.

EWALD: That's true. Of course I shouldn't have done it.

HELEN: Oh yes, yes.

EWALD: No. And I realize, too, that I shouldn't have dragged you into all this mess here.

HELEN: In the course of time I've learned to know what's good for me.

EWALD: There are things that one should cope with alone.

HELEN: You're talking with your own voice, but it sounds to me as if someone is standing behind you and telling you what to say. But you are not like that. You are not as stuffy and unimpeachable and dry as people think you are. You are a connoisseur of wine. You have a sense of humor. Now I know. But you hide yourself. Why?

EWALD: It's time for you to go home. *(Looks at his watch)* It's quite late already.

HELEN: I live in a flat and I'm my own boss.

EWALD: You have to go.

HELEN: All right.

EWALD: I still have something to do at the lab but first I'll see you home. I've left the car outside.

HELEN: It looks as if you've figured it all out beforehand. Picking mushrooms, Lafitte '72, and then seeing me home.

EWALD: *(Sharply)* Shut up!

HELEN: Oh, I don't mind at all. I want you to see me home.

EWALD: Listen . . . As long as Jeanne refuses a reasonable divorce we must be very careful.

HELEN: So you are the man you want people to think you are. And for one moment I thought you were different.

EWALD: You don't know what you're talking about.

HELEN: Oh, yes. I know quite well. What will the colleagues say? My scientific career is at stake. These damned toadstools are more important to you than I am. *(Starts weeping)*

EWALD: The British laws on divorce are extremely hard on the wage-earning male of the marital unit.

HELEN: I didn't mean it. It's because of the wine. I'm sorry.

EWALD: *(Caressing her)* You don't need to apologize, but I assure you, you don't know what you're talking about. It's a deep and difficult problem, but soon there'll be a solution.

HELEN: What are we going to do now?

EWALD: I'll see you home and then I'll drive on to the lab. Eriksen asked me expressly to drop the proofs in his box tomorrow and you know that tomorrow I haven't a single moment to spare.

HELEN: Yes, I do. It's my job to know that. It's all written on the pages of my notebook. I'm a very good assistant. Not only do I know a lot about mushrooms, but I manage your appointments in an extremely efficient way. Nothing ever goes wrong.

EWALD: We'll talk about it tomorrow.

HELEN: Tomorrow I'll be too much ashamed to look at you.

EWALD: Oh no. Tomorrow everything will be all right.

HELEN: I could kill her.

EWALD: You weren't going to say that again.

HELEN: I don't care.

EWALD: Shall we go?

HELEN: All right.

EWALD: Tomorrow everything will be different.

HELEN: Everything is always different tomorrow.

(EWALD looks around him, puts the wine bottle and the empty wine glasses together with books and papers in his briefcase and goes. HELEN follows him.

As soon as they have gone JEANNE appears. She goes to the pot with the mushrooms, looks carefully at them, sniffs. Meanwhile the door opens and ALBERT enters. JEANNE starts, shocked)

ALBERT: It's only me. You don't have to be afraid. I heard a car. *(Looks around)* Where are they?

JEANNE: Gone.

ALBERT: What do you mean? Dead?

JEANNE: He is seeing her home.

ALBERT: *(Frightened)* That was them?

JEANNE: Yes.

ALBERT: For a moment I was scared that, pickled as you are, you had hauled the stiffs into the car to stow them away somewhere.

JEANNE: I'm not drunk.

COMMERCIAL TRAVELLER: *(Enters, furious)* What does this mean?

JEANNE: What do you mean?

CT: I've been watching, waiting to see a doctor's car arrive and after that a police car, but I saw your husband and his assistant driving away. *(Explodes again)* What does this mean?

JEANNE: I don't know. I have no idea.

CT: What kind of damned, unforgivable, woolly-headed stupidity have you been up to?

JEANNE: Don't behave like this to me, sir.

CT: *(Breathes deeply and recovers)* I beg your pardon. You're my client. I must have been beside myself with rage. I'm not used to it. This is the first time in my career as a broker that a thing like this has happened to me. This is a tremendous shock and you will understand that my usual equanimity has been disturbed for a brief moment. I hope you'll forgive me.

JEANNE: It's all right. I understand how shocked you must have been. Imagine what I felt when I came in and saw the two turtle-doves coming in from the garden. For a moment I thought I saw ghosts.

CT: I regret to say they were not. Something must have gone wrong, though your part in the proceedings was simple enough.

JEANNE: I did everything just as you told me. The telephone. That was all right. And then luring away that girl. That went just as you predicted, too.

CT: Of course. Go on, please.

ALBERT: It's me who put that mushroom into the stew.

CT: *(Amazed)* Which mushroom?

ALBERT: *(Goes to the bookcase, looks in the book)* This one.

CT: *(Looks)* The real Pseudo. Where did you get that?

ALBERT: That's my business.

CT: I see. Perhaps I underestimated you. The real goods, eh? *(With relish)* Perhaps you did make a mistake. As I said, amateurs should stick to cricket or ballet, and not meddle in murder.

ALBERT: I'm no amateur.

CT: *(Shrugs his shoulders)* Things have gone wrong, haven't they?

JEANNE: What now?

CT: *(Goes to the cooking corner)* Are these the remnants of the meal?

JEANNE: Yes.

CT: You're sure they have eaten from this pan?

JEANNE: Yes, more than half of it.

CT: *(Sniffs)* It looks good. Smells good, too. As a matter of fact, I'm a great lover of well-seasoned fungi. *(Lifts a bit to his mouth, then drops it)* No, better not. *(Picks up the Pseudo from the pan. To* ALBERT) Here it is, sir, your contribution to the scheme. Yes, it really looks like a Pseudo. Something very strange must've happened. I'll take a sample of this to our laboratories for inspection. It might be one of the very rare mutations, that looks like Pseudoes, but is not. Pseudo Pseudoes one could call them. Have you got a bag for me? Plastic? Thank you.

ALBERT: *(Shamefully)* I got it from the Professor himself, with certificate and all.

CT: From the best expert in the world? That makes it even stranger. Well, people are never to be trusted. In our business you must always and exclusively rely on yourself.

ALBERT: *(With a hint of admiration)* You're right. That's what I always say, too.

(Telephone light goes on)

JEANNE: Someone on the phone. *(Looks quizzically at CT)*

CT: It's better to answer. *(Exit* JEANNE. *To* ALBERT) A fine mess you've made of it.

ALBERT: *(Nervously)* I can't understand it.

CT: But I can. In this branch of the profession you're an amateur. I hope you've learned your lesson. I won't stand any more interference from you. From now on you do what I say, otherwise there are some very nasty surprises in store for you. Do you understand what I mean?

ALBERT: *(After a long internal struggle of indignation, rage and then submission)* Yes, I do.

CT: Fine. Now we can do business together.

JEANNE: *(Entering, to* ALBERT*)* It's for you.

ALBERT: Who?

JEANNE: He wouldn't give his name.

ALBERT: *(Astonished)* Who can that be? *(Exit)*

CT: "What now" you just asked, didn't you?

JEANNE: *(Nervously)* Yes.

CT: *(Looking searchingly at her)* Anyway, that's a sign of a great spirit of enterprise. You don't feel any remorse for what you intended to do?

JEANNE: No.

CT: Are you disappointed with our failure?

JEANNE: Yes.

CT: Your tenacity does you credit.

JEANNE: Why?

ALBERT: A little job. It's urgent. *(Kisses* JEANNE *perfunctorily)* I'll be back soon. *(To CT)* See you later, too, sir.

CT: Is it that urgent that we can't finish our conversation?

ALBERT: *(Nervously)* Yes. Very urgent. But I won't be long. *(Exit)*

JEANNE: I wonder what it is he has to do so suddenly.

CT: I think one of his former associates must've phoned him with a nasty message, urging him to leave, rather than to attend our strategy talk.

JEANNE: How do you know that?

CT: That's the advantage of belonging to a big organization. We know very much about our clients. Very much, indeed.

JEANNE: I'd rather he stayed.

CT: It's better this way.

JEANNE: *(Surprised)* You wanted him to go away.

CT: He's rather conceited and apt to act on his own impulses and insight. In our business, however, private enterprise is disastrous. So you want to go on?

JEANNE: Yes.

CT: Under the same conditions?

JEANNE: Yes.

CT: Good. Then you'll have to listen carefully.

JEANNE: Do you have another plan already?

CT: Yes, and nothing can go wrong this time, providing you adhere meticulously to my instructions.

JEANNE: You're right. I promise.

CT: We must act now on the spur of the moment, our initial plan being wrecked by our ingenious friend. But I've always a second solution in mind when planning a campaign. I think that this time suicide might be more appropriate than the fateful mistake of a famous mycologist.

JEANNE: Suicide, but why . . . *(Reflectingly)* Well, now that you mention it, he has been rather depressed lately.

CT: I know. Marked moods of depression have been noticed by his immediate associates at the lab during the last two months.

JEANNE: I didn't know that.

CT: Yes, suicide could be made extremely convincing.

JEANNE: Then his secretary could testify that he suffered from depression?

CT: *(After a long silence)* I'm sure she will, Madam.

JEANNE: *(Musingly)* Suicide.

CT: For the police sleeping pills are always the most convincing means of voluntary death.

JEANNE: Sleeping pills. He's been taking them recently. He's been very nervous. They're in his desk. *(Looks)* Here they are.

CT: Sleeping pills as such are unreliable. Sometimes they work as they ought to and sometimes they don't. We have to leave the impression that he has taken too many pills and in the meantime we have to give him more effective medicine, which, of course, is a well-known tool of the trade in our profession. It's completely tasteless and odorless.

JEANNE: Not the real stuff?

CT: No, a better one.

JEANNE: But how can we give it to him, so that it looks as if he has taken it himself? *(Slaps her forehead)* Of course, how stupid of me to forget. He always drinks black coffee when he has to work, and for the last few weeks that has been every night. In the coffee. He asked me to make a thermos flask full. Sometimes he does it himself, but I do it better and therefore he keeps asking me to make it for him. —Wait a minute. *(Listens)* Yes.

CT: What's the matter?

JEANNE: Just a moment. *(Listens again)* It's the sound of his car.

CT: His car? That's impossible,. He has just left. You must be mistaken.

JEANNE: No, I know that sound too well. *(Listens)* Yes, now he's near the garage. He should be here in a moment. *(In panic)* What can we do?

CT: Stay calm. Don't worry.

JEANNE: Let's go to the drawing room. Yes, he's already at the door. Come! *(She puts out the light. Vague light comes through the glass in the garden door. CT and JEANNE exit. EWALD enters through the garden door, puts on the light, inspects the room, then opens the hall door.)*

EWALD: Jeanne! Jeanne!

JEANNE: *(Entering)* What's the matter? What are you doing here?

EWALD: On my way to the lab I realized that I had forgotten Preston's Handbook of Fungi of the British Isles. I absolutely must have it, but I can't find it. Have you seen it anywhere?

JEANNE: Me? No. For that matter, I don't even know what the damned thing looks like.

EWALD: A big, thick book about this size. *(Indicates)* With a brown cover.

JEANNE: No, I really haven't the slightest idea.

EWALD: I must have it, or I can't go on with my work.

JEANNE: It doesn't very often happen than you can't find something.

EWALD: I haven't come back only for Preston's Handbook of the Fungi of the British Isles.

JEANNE: That doesn't surprise me at all. What do you want?

EWALD: I wanted to have one last talk with you.

JEANNE: We've talked more than enough already.

EWALD: I want to talk again.

JEANNE: You know my conditions.

EWALD: You know that I don't earn enough for them.

JEANNE: That's not my problem. It's you who is asking. When the price is too steep, don't buy.

EWALD: It's unjust.

JEANNE: It's the law.

EWALD: Some laws are so unfair that breaking them is a form of justice.

JEANNE: The law is the law.

EWALD: I'll give you what I can spare.

JEANNE: That's not enough.

EWALD: What do you get out of staying with me?

JEANNE: More than I can get out of a divorce on your terms. There's your pension. And in case you should die unexpectedly, there's your life insurance.

EWALD: Don't go too far.

JEANNE: I know exactly how far I can go.

EWALD: Is that your last word?

JEANNE: Yes.

EWALD: Good. Will you remember the coffee?

JEANNE: I won't forget it. *(Exit through the hall door)*

(EWALD goes through the garden door, then turns. He goes to the bookcase. From behind the Collected Works of Pope he takes the bottle of whisky and takes a good swig out of it. With his back to the audience he returns the bottle, then exits through the garden door.

A moment later JEANNE and CT appear, entering through the hall door. In the distance, the sound of an engine starting is heard.)

CT: Let's hope he doesn't forget another important book.

JEANNE: No. One is enough for him. Anyway, he seldom forgets anything.

CT: In any case we must prepare our second attempt as soon as possible. It must be tonight.

JEANNE: So soon?

CT: Yes. A homicide postponed too long is apt to start stinking.

JEANNE: And if it goes wrong again this time?

CT: Then we'll have to drop it. In our business the third time does not do the trick, but is just one too many. It's clear what we have to do. Life has become a burden, too heavy for your husband to bear. There are his difficulties at home; a deeply hidden, unhappy love for a young woman in his proximity; a general disgust with life. Tonight your husband will commit suicide out of despair. *(Taking a powder from his pocket)* Here's the powder. It works much quicker than the pills. Concentrated sleeping pills one could say. Especially manufactured for our firm. It's essential for our plan. Your husband drinks the coffee. He gets sleepy and lies down on the couch as he usually does. He falls into a deep sleep. He dies a soft, I might say, an enviable death. *(Silence)*

JEANNE: Let me think it over. He drinks the coffee and then lies down on the couch.

CT: One hour later you enter the room. *(He indicates the following steps of his plan, counting on his fingers to make it clear to* JEANNE*)* Then you put a glass of water here on the table in which you have dissolved a considerable number of these sleeping pills. You empty the glass in the sink, but you take care some of the mixture is left. This will facilitate the police investigation. Then you take the thermos flask with the coffee and clean it carefully in the kitchen so that no trace of the powder will be left.

JEANNE: Is that all?

CT: Yes. And now, to get it straight, a rehearsal.

JEANNE: Another rehearsal?

CT: Yes, I always do that, and it's a wise habit, if I may say so. So I'm your husband now, I come home and sit down to do a little work. Suddenly I'd like to have a cup of good strong coffee. Immediately afterwards I feel sleepy, and probably I'll lie down on the couch. *(He does it)* Never to rise again. *(He rises immediately)* You enter now.

JEANNE: I enter.

CT: Fine. And what do you do now?

JEANNE: I take the sleeping pills and the glass. *(She starts to do so)*

CT: No, no, one moment. You can do that later. Take care not to leave fingerprints on it. You can use a dish-cloth.

JEANNE: So I take a glass and dissolve the sleeping pills in it. Then I throw the water away in the sink here, but take care that something remains in the glass. I put it here on the table. I take the thermos flask to the kitchen to clean it carefully. *(She has mimed all these gestures)*

CT: Exactly. Then nature, aided by human ingenuity, does its work. *(Silence)* The events are tied together by such a strict logical framework that nothing can go wrong.

JEANNE: Are you sure?

CT: Absolutely sure.

JEANNE: Good. *(She goes toward the bookcase)*

CT: What are you doing now?

JEANNE: I'd like a little snifter.

CT: No. Not now. When the coffee is ready. Not before. Go and prepare it. The sooner it's over, the better. In this case drinking can have the same fatal effect as when you're driving a car. You must keep your head clear and your hand steady.

JEANNE: You're right. I once nearly killed a child on the road.

CT: I know.

JEANNE: *(Nervous)* That, too?

CT: Yes. I wish you luck, madam. I hope to see you soon for the last time. For the settlement.

(When he has gone, JEANNE stares after him for a few moments. She hesitatingly goes to the bookcase. Then firmly she puts out the light. Only a small desk lamp remains. She takes the thermos flask and exits

through the hall door. The stage remains empty for a few moments.

Then CT *enters again, through the garden door and makes a sign with a pocket flashlight)*

CT: Come in. Quickly. You have exactly two minutes. No more.

(ALBERT *enters. He can be seen clearly in the beam from the flashlight.* CT *gives him gloves, which he puts on.* ALBERT *goes to the shelf where the bottle of poison extract, which* JEANNE *has mentioned to him in the first act stands, then goes to the bookcase and reaches behind the books where the whisky bottle must be.)*

[END OF ACT II]

Act Three

(The next morning. HELEN, *the assistant, is present but now without spectacles and in smarter clothes. She looks remarkably more handsome. It could even be called a metamorphosis. She is moving around, looking up things in books and making notes.*

The INSPECTOR *enters.)*

INSPECTOR: You're earlier than the birds.

HELEN: *(Startled)* Yes, work must go on.

INSPECTOR: *(Melancholically)* I know. Work must always go on. I've had to work the whole night through because two pimps nearly chopped each other's heads off. You would think that after something like that you would have a little rest for the night, and then you are called out of your nest again because someone has taken too many dreampills. It's a fine job. A calling. I don't complain. But why does a murder or a suicide or something like that, always have to happen outside the official office hours? That's what I can't understand.

HELEN: I don't know, Inspector.

INSPECTOR: It was not a question, miss, it was merely blowing off steam in the early morning. *(Looks at his watch)* Oh well, in a few minutes I'll hop between the old blankets again. This is a very simple case. *(Suddenly starts)* You're not one of the relatives, I take it.

HELEN: No, not at all. I'm only the professor's assistant.

INSPECTOR: All right. *(Looks in his note book)* You are the one who rang me up?

HELEN: No . . . I . . . I have . . .

INSPECTOR: No, that's true, it was a man's voice. But now that we're here I might as well ask you some more questions. *(Sits)* You may sit down, Miss . . . eh . . . eh . . .

HELEN: Engels. Helen Engels.

INSPECTOR: Miss Engels. It makes talking easier.

HELEN: *(Sitting)* What do you want to know? I've told you already how I found the body.

INSPECTOR: *(Looks at her searchingly)* You give the impression of not being too disturbed by it all.

HELEN: I didn't have much friendly contact with the deceased.

INSPECTOR: Most people are more or less disturbed when they discover a corpse, especially so early in the morning.

HELEN: As a rule I have my feelings quite under control, Inspector. *(Short silence)* That's part of my work.

INSPECTOR: Of course. Such people do exist. Only you don't meet them too often. It's a policeman's duty to wonder whenever there's a reason, and even when there's no reason at all. It never does any harm.

HELEN: I can imagine that, Inspector.

INSPECTOR: Anyhow, it's not important here. I wish every case I had to handle was so simple.

HELEN: That didn't keep you from being very careful in your investigations, Inspector. Photos, fingerprints.

INSPECTOR: Routine. Pure routine, Miss. *(Takes a pen)* But may I have your story now? You arrived here this morning.

HELEN: At nine o'clock.

INSPECTOR: Exactly?

HELEN: Exactly. I had an appointment with the Professor to call on him at nine to talk over something before we went to the laboratory, and I am used to keeping my appointments very strictly.

INSPECTOR: Isn't that a bit unusual, that an assistant picks up her employer to go with him to work?

HELEN: No.

INSPECTOR: *(Dripping with friendliness)* Can't you explain that a little more clearly?

HELEN: I don't see what it has to do with this case.

INSPECTOR: You might leave that to me. It's my job. *(Silence)*

HELEN: All right. The Professor doesn't like to drive . . . and in this room here he does a lot of work. I often call for him. Then I sort out the mess he has made, and I take care that the experiments he has prepared here can be executed in the laboratory.

INSPECTOR: Very understandable. And does that happen often?

HELEN: That depends on the work.

INSPECTOR: You do a lot of work in the evening, too?

HELEN: Yes.

INSPECTOR: So you work harder than you have to.

HELEN: I like doing it.

INSPECTOR: For the work?

HELEN: For the work.

INSPECTOR: Of course. For the work. That's why I'm on my way so early, too. For the work. You were present when the body was found, weren't you?

HELEN: Yes.

INSPECTOR: Have you moved anything?

HELEN: Oh, yes, At first I thought it would be possible to do something.

INSPECTOR: *(Writing)* But it was no use?

HELEN: No. I soon saw that.

INSPECTOR: Did you put the body on the couch?

HELEN: I helped.

INSPECTOR: It must have been quite a weight.

HELEN: I'm strong.

INSPECTOR: You don't look it.

HELEN: There's a lot you can't see at first sight.

INSPECTOR: Where did the body lie exactly?

HELEN: *(Going to the place)* Here. Near the chair.

INSPECTOR: *(Making notes)* Strange, when you think of it. The deceased prepared the final drink, wanting to die sitting. That's strange. Most people, seeking a voluntary death, want to die lying, as if they were going to sleep. If I had done something like that I would've lain down on the couch.

HELEN: Everyone has his own way of dying.

INSPECTOR: Perhaps you don't realize how right you are, Miss . . . uh . . . uh . . .

HELEN: Engels.

INSPECTOR: Miss Engels. If I need a secretary, and if you are free, I'd like to have you.

HELEN: I'll keep that in mind, Inspector.

INSPECTOR: Besides that you left everything exactly as it was?

HELEN: Yes.

INSPECTOR: Have you any idea what the reason for this suicide could be?

HELEN: *(Emphatically)* No. Not at all.

INSPECTOR: I only asked. It's part of my work. After all, you were closely associated with the Professor. You might've noticed something.

HELEN: No. I haven't noticed anything.

INSPECTOR: *(Writes and murmurs)* Assistant . . . noticed . . . nothing . . .

EWALD: *(Entering, has heard the last words of the Inspector)* Perhaps I can help you, Inspector.

INSPECTOR: Ah, Professor. Have you recovered well enough from the shock for me to ask you a few questions?

EWALD: It was quite a shock indeed. *(He breathes deeply and sits down)* Nevertheless I'm prepared to answer your questions.

HELEN: Have you had coffee already?

INSPECTOR: No thank you. I won't have to bother you much longer. The case is nearly rounded off. I only need a little more information.

EWALD: I'm at your service.

INSPECTOR: At what time did you discover the accident, Professor?

HELEN: I told you already.

INSPECTOR: I'd like to hear it from the Professor himself.

EWALD: At nine o'clock exactly.

INSPECTOR: How do you remember it so precisely?

EWALD: My assistant is extremely meticulous. She is always exactly on time. I myself am a little sloppy in this respect. I always notice the time of her arrival. It has become a habit with me. I think that unconsciously I'm waiting for her to make a mistake.

INSPECTOR: And till now she hasn't made one?

EWALD: Until now, no.

INSPECTOR: It will happen. Nobody is infallible. But all right, it was on the stroke of nine. Tell me, Professor, what happened.

EWALD: I had gone to bed late and fallen asleep immediately. At a quarter to nine I awoke and I was hardly dressed when Helen . . . uh . . . Miss Engels rang the bell.

INSPECTOR: Where do you sleep?

EWALD: My wife and I have had separate bedrooms for some time.

INSPECTOR: Marital problems?

EWALD: Yes.

INSPECTOR: I understand. Go on, please.

EWALD: I went downstairs and opened the door for Miss Engels. We had something to do in my study and went in together. We immediately saw the   the   the body.

INSPECTOR: Death must've taken place in the early hours of the morning. Didn't you notice anything, Professor?

EWALD: No.

INSPECTOR: Doesn't that strike you as strange?

EWALD: My bedroom is on the upper floor.

INSPECTOR: At what time did your wife usually get up?

EWALD: It varied considerably.

INSPECTOR: Did you use to have breakfast together?

EWALD: During the last few months we seldom saw each other before dinner. She has been very depressed, lately.

INSPECTOR: Depressed?

EWALD: Yes.

INSPECTOR: Was there any special reason for it?

EWALD: No special reason, as far as I could see, but she has been very nervous, difficult to get along with.

INSPECTOR: That happens in most marriages. Marriage, Professor, is the best way to test man's capacity for living together.

EWALD: *(Coolly)* Yes, of course, I quite agree.

INSPECTOR: But that's no reason to go to the end of the road.

EWALD: Sometimes it does happen. This time, for instance.

INSPECTOR: Yes, obviously. *(Walking around)* Why here, I wonder.

EWALD: I don't know.

INSPECTOR: This is your study, isn't it?

EWALD: Yes.

INSPECTOR: A man's study. The masculine touch, you know. Rational, well-kept and yet untidy. It lacks the cosy uselessness of a female's tender hand.

EWALD: I didn't know, Inspector, that the police force was such a breeding ground for romantic rot.

INSPECTOR: There are a lot of things you don't know outside your specialism, Professor.

EWALD: *(Is startled, looks at him suspiciously)* You're quite right, Inspector.

INSPECTOR: So why here?

EWALD: I asked her to prepare some coffee for me. I often work at night.

INSPECTOR: Well, let's leave that for the moment. *(To* HELEN*)* You were present when the body was found?

HELEN: Yes, I have told you that already.

INSPECTOR: *(To* EWALD*)* You laid the body on the couch?

EWALD: Together with Miss Engels. It was rather heavy.

INSPECTOR: Didn't you think it strange that the body was lying by that chair in the middle of the room?

EWALD: It didn't enter my mind.

INSPECTOR: *(Quickly to* HELEN*)* And you?

HELEN: Mine neither.

INSPECTOR: It looks as if little reflection has been lost among all the people concerned with this case.

HELEN: It must have been an act of despair. And then you don't reflect.

INSPECTOR: I have more experience in these things than you have, Miss. To each his own profession, I always say. There's something wrong here. *(Silence)*

EWALD: What, Inspector?

INSPECTOR: There is a contradiction between the position of the body here on the floor and the kind of poison used in this presumable act of despair. It's all far too premeditated.

EWALD: You already know the cause of death?

INSPECTOR: Yes.

EWALD: Sleeping pills, of course.

INSPECTOR: Why do you think that?

EWALD: It's obvious, isn't it?

INSPECTOR: Nothing is obvious with regard to a sudden death, Professor.

HELEN: Isn't that a little exaggerated, Inspector?

INSPECTOR: *(Turning suddenly to her)* No. I know what I am talking about. I've handled hundreds of similar cases. There's always a certain kind of pattern in them. I don't see that pattern here. *(Silence)*

EWALD: What now?

INSPECTOR: We'll see. So you immediately called the police?

EWALD: Yes.

INSPECTOR: Where?

EWALD: In the drawing room. That's where the telephone is.

INSPECTOR: Why haven't you got an extension here?

EWALD: I don't want to be disturbed when I'm working.

INSPECTOR: Yes, I can imagine that. I wish that I could say the same, but they call me in the middle of the night. When did you have this telephone light installed?

EWALD: Some months ago.

INSPECTOR: *(Reflectingly)* I see. A good idea. Pity I can't use it. Be glad you're not an inspector, Professor.

EWALD: To each his own profession, Inspector.

INSPECTOR: That's true. So you went to the telephone and Miss Engels stayed here.

EWALD: Yes.

INSPECTOR: And you haven't moved anything?

EWALD: No.

INSPECTOR: You haven't cleaned or washed anything?

HELEN: No. This is ridiculous.

EWALD: Inspector, will you be so kind as to tell us exactly what is the matter?

INSPECTOR: *(Goes to the cooking corner and takes a glass)* This glass has been washed by someone. Hastily and badly, I must confess, but still it has been tampered with. *(To* EWALD*)* Can you find an explanation for this, Professor?

EWALD: I? Uh . . . No.

EWALD: You're sure?

EWALD: Yes.

INSPECTOR: And you, Miss Engels, are you sure that you haven't washed this glass? Out of a kind of habit, for instance? It is a fact that people under heavy tension often maintain their old habits. Something like that could've been the case with you.

HELEN: *(Sharply)* I know quite well what I've done and what I haven't done, Inspector. And I haven't touched that glass at all.

INSPECTOR: Then someone else must've done it. We'll find out.

EWALD: How?

INSPECTOR: There are some fine fingerprints on that glass.

HELEN: And you told us that it had been washed.

INSPECTOR: Yes, but badly. The prints are as clear as sunshine. Fingerprints, Miss Engels are often stronger than water.

EWALD: There's one thing you seem to neglect, Inspector.

INSPECTOR: What is it, Professor? I'm an old hand in the profession, but one can always learn a thing or two.

EWALD: That my wife could've washed the glass herself.

INSPECTOR: That's impossible, Professor.

EWALD: What?

INSPECTOR: We found another glass in this room that was standing here on the table. *(Takes it out of his briefcase and puts it on the table)* This glass, in which there were still some drops of whisky left, has been investigated by our experts. Your wife's fingerprints were on this glass. A superficial comparison showed that the fingerprints on this glass *(Points to the other glass)* were *not* those of your wife. My Manual of Basic Steps in Crime Detection teaches me that they must be someone else's.

EWALD: And whose might those be?

INSPECTOR: That's what we are ferreting out at the moment. We'll know soon. There's a big organization behind us, you must remember.

EWALD: What does it all mean?

INSPECTOR: It means that your wife must have been murdered, Professor.

HELEN: Murdered? Oh God!

EWALD: Murdered? Impossible!

INSPECTOR: Experience has taught me that murder is always possible.

EWALD: And who murdered her then?

INSPECTOR: It's my profession to root that out. Do you miss anything in this room, Professor?

EWALD: *(Looking around)* No, nothing.

INSPECTOR: Will you be so kind as to look on that shelf?

EWALD: My God, the extract of Pseudomirabellus! *(He takes the bottle, half of it is gone)*

INSPECTOR: It was full, wasn't it?

EWALD: Yes. *(Amazed)* How do you know?

INSPECTOR: A simple analysis of the cork.

HELEN: You've done your work extremely thoroughly, Inspector.

INSPECTOR: Honest work deserves to be done as well as possible, Miss Engels. A very strong poison, isn't it, Professor? Nobody knows better than you that this extract is tasteless, odorless and deadly, even when administered in very small quantities. Well, Professor, the investigation is not yet finished, but we can already say with certainty that the glass which held the remnants of whisky and had your wife's fingerprints contained this poison.

HELEN: It's impossible! Ewald, tell him it's not true.

INSPECTOR: These are the facts, Miss Engels. *(To* EWALD*)* You were on somewhat of a bad footing with your wife, weren't you, Professor?

EWALD: That's preposterous. How dare you!

INSPECTOR: I'm here to ask the questions, not to answer them. To each man his own profession, Professor. *(To* HELEN*)* And you've been on very good terms with the Professor, haven't you, Miss Engels?

EWALD: I beg you to leave my assistant alone.

INSPECTOR: If possible I'd like to, Professor. The only question is whether it is possible.

EWALD: What do you mean?

INSPECTOR: I'm only a simple Police Inspector. They called me to a simple suicide case. I find some simple deviations. These simple deviations show up in a simple situation: a man, a wife, another woman. What should I, as a simple policeman, think of that?

HELEN: That's sheer nonsense. The Professor and I found her together.

INSPECTOR: Who's word do I have for it? Only yours and the Professor's.

HELEN: So you don't believe us.

INSPECTOR: I believe in facts.

EWALD: Are you accusing us?

INSPECTOR: No.

HELEN: Then why are you saying all these things?

INSPECTOR: To frighten you a bit.

EWALD: Why?

INSPECTOR: Because I want to know the truth. Up to now you haven't told it. *(Long silence. The telephone light goes on.* EWALD *starts to go)* No, you stay here. I'll take the telephone. I think it's for me. I've given orders to Headquarters to ring me immediately when they have some news. *(Exit)*

HELEN: What's that man up to?

EWALD: I don't know.

HELEN: He makes me nervous.

EWALD: There's no reason for that.

HELEN: I know, but he still makes me nervous.

EWALD: When you're sure that you don't need to be afraid, it's not necessary to be afraid.

HELEN: What a strange thing to say.

EWALD: It's the truth.

HELEN: I'd like to know what that man knows.

EWALD: He knows what the facts have told him.

HELEN: *(Bursting out)* For God's sake, Ewald, stop it! I can't stand it any longer. *(He goes to her to console her)*

EWALD: It's only for a short time. When it's all over we can have a new life.

HELEN: That Inspector frightens me.

EWALD: After all, an Inspector is only an official.

HELEN: He's smarter than you think.

EWALD: But he's an official and that means that he sees the facts as he has learned to see them; and that's why you don't need to be afraid.

HELEN: I try, but I can't. *(Walks to and fro agitatedly)* We must tell him.

EWALD: No, no, we promised.

HELEN: We must. It's useless to hide it anymore.

EWALD: Now that she's dead it's even more necessary.

HELEN: That Inspector suspects something.

EWALD: Let him suspect.

(INSPECTOR enters, reflectively. He takes the glasses from the table, looks at them contemplatively for a long time and then puts them back.)

INSPECTOR: A very interesting telephone conversation.

EWALD: What was it?

INSPECTOR: The unknown fingerprints on the glass have been identified.

EWALD: Whose are they?

INSPECTOR: They are from a well-known petty thief who has been in Her Majesty's care several times for a couple of months. Mostly for blackmail. *(Silence)*

EWALD: So that's it.

INSPECTOR: Yes. Will you now be so kind as to tell the truth, Professor?

EWALD: My wife was being blackmailed.

INSPECTOR: That's what I already suspected.

EWALD: I presume you also know why?

INSPECTOR: We can guess it from the crime sheet of the man in question.

EWALD: He must've been her lover.

INSPECTOR: Little fantasy is necessary to imagine that. That little crook has blackmailed many women by threatening to withdraw his love from them. Withdrawal of affection is a powerful weapon in the extortion business.

EWALD: *(Musingly)* Yes, love is a powerful drive.

INSPECTOR: What you've told me gives me the impression that you must've known before.

EWALD: Even someone like me must have his suspicions. To think that I myself offered him hospitality. We met him on a holiday trip. In the beginning I rather liked him.

INSPECTOR: And you did nothing about it?

EWALD: I had no proof. They were very careful.

INSPECTOR: How did she get the money?

EWALD: She had some of her own. She must have spent that.

Now and then I gave her something. Not often.

INSPECTOR: *(Stupefied)* What did you say?

EWALD: Yes, sometimes I felt sorry for her. *(Long silence)*

INSPECTOR: Even when you suspected what she needed it for?

EWALD: Yes.

INSPECTOR: In my profession I come up occasionally against people who stand in front of me just like you're doing now and yet who leave the impression of not existing at all. You are such a man. My common sense tells me softness has no limits, but my feelings make me suspicious. Can you imagine that?

EWALD: Yes.

INSPECTOR: Thank you.

EWALD: I know that it must sound strange but it's the truth.

INSPECTOR: No, Professor, it's not the truth. At least, not the whole truth. I accept the fact that you pitied your wife, however strange it might sound, but for me the case still isn't finished. There are still too many contradictions to solve. *(Counts them on his fingers)* The position of the body, the washed-out whisky glass, the half-empty poison bottle, all that could point to a murder. But blackmailers as a rule are not murderers, for, Professor, dead people can't pay.

EWALD: *(Under heavy stress)* I murdered her! *(Long silence)*

HELEN: *(Screams)* No, no, it's not true!

INSPECTOR: Will you be so kind as to be a bit more explicit, Professor? How, when, why?

EWALD: She must've been desperate, so desperate she even asked me for money. *(Silence)* I refused her. *(Silence)*

INSPECTOR: Did she tell you why she needed the money?

EWALD: No, and I didn't ask her, either. I didn't want to know. She was mad with fear, but I refused her the money. It must've driven her to her death, but I couldn't spare it. I had drawn out the last of what I had in the bank. To pay off the mortgage. The installment was already overdue.

INSPECTOR: How much was it?

EWALD: Four hundred pounds.

INSPECTOR: A tidy little sum.

EWALD: She stole it.

INSPECTOR: *(Jumping up)* What's that you say?

EWALD: Yes, today I had an appointment with my solicitor. But the money isn't there any more. *(Goes to his desk)* Here are the papers. The last payment on the house

INSPECTOR: Thank you. I believe you.

EWALD: Blackmailers are insatiable. They always demand more. I presume that she didn't see any way out. I murdered her with my refusal.

INSPECTOR: Not in the sense of the law, Professor. Furthermore I must inform you that the money is no longer in the house.

HELEN: Have you looked that carefully, Inspector?

INSPECTOR: Yes, Miss Engels, that's part of the profession.

EWALD: Then she must've given it to him already.

INSPECTOR: Pity. It would be nice if we could catch the blackmailer with the evidence, but a good craftsman always takes care that there is no evidence.

EWALD: This time there is. I've copied the numbers of the notes.

INSPECTOR: *(Suspiciously)* Why?

EWALD: Just an old habit. I'm not very good at handling money. I often lose it. I don't mind very much when it's a matter of small sums, but for bigger ones I do. Hence the habit.

INSPECTOR: Extremely clever. And it comes in extraordinarily handy, too, May I copy the numbers from you? *(Writes)* Thank you. Well, the case is over, now.

HELEN: At last!

INSPECTOR: But for one tiny detail, of course. *(Silence)* The coffee in the thermos flask was poisoned, too.

HELEN: No!

INSPECTOR: For whom was that coffee intended?

EWALD: For me. *(Amazed)* But that would mean ...

INSPECTOR: Just so. That your wife wanted to poison you. She wanted to murder you, and then someone else made her see the darkness of eternity.

EWALD: That blackmailer.

INSPECTOR: Or you.

EWALD: *(Jumping up)* What are you saying?

INSPECTOR: You could've done it, too.

EWALD: What kind of madness is this?

INSPECTOR: No madness at all, but the result of logical thinking. An eye for an eye, a tooth for a tooth. He who digs a hole for another will fall into one himself. Very truthful proverb, sir. Your wife wanted to poison you with coffee. You poisoned her with whisky.

EWALD: How?

INSPECTOR: By giving her poisoned whisky to drink.

EWALD: When?

INSPECTOR: Between then and now. It doesn't matter so much. Besides, you had the whole night to do it. The doctor's report says that your wife must have died between one and three in the morning.

HELEN: I'm going to tell him.

EWALD: No!

HELEN: Don't you see that we can't keep it secret any longer?

INSPECTOR: Tell me, Miss Engels. We're bound to get at the truth eventually.

HELEN: Professor Harewood can't have done it.

INSPECTOR: Why not?

HELEN: He spent the night with me. *(Silence)*

INSPECTOR: So. With you.

HELEN: Yes.

INSPECTOR: *(To* EWALD*)* Your bed was undisturbed. I asked myself where you could've been last night. It increased my suspicions. But naturally the statement of your assistant is of the utmost importance. *(To* HELEN*)* So you came here together this morning?

HELEN: Yes.

INSPECTOR: Can you prove that?

HELEN: I think so. My neighbors are of the new-fashioned kind, very tolerant and very inquisitive. I'm sure they could give you a report on my conduct from minute to minute.

INSPECTOR: Of course I'll have to interrogate them as a matter of routine, but for the time being I take it this is the truth.

HELEN: It is.

INSPECTOR: You came into the house together, too?

HELEN: No, I waited in the car. The Professor, Ewald, had to get his galley proofs. A few minutes later he came back upset and told me that something had happened. Then I went with him into the house.

INSPECTOR: *(To* EWALD*)* How long were you alone?

EWALD: Only a couple of minutes. When I entered the study I saw immediately my . . . eh . . . wife lying there. I called Helen straight away.

INSPECTOR: Her testimony, if proven true, is your salvation, Professor.

EWALD: Did you really suspect me?

INSPECTOR: Yes.

EWALD: Why?

INSPECTOR: Because I have the impression that a sharp, even a powerful mind has been at work here; brains, being able to think with a sound, analytical precision. You've got brains of that quality, Professor. *(He hears a sound and looks outside)* Somebody's coming. It's better for him not to see you. Will you, please, go into the drawing room and wait until I give you a sign?

(HELEN and EWALD exit. A few moments of silence. ALBERT opens the garden door. He sees the INSPECTOR, looks surprised, and then smiles)

ALBERT: Top o' the morning to you!

INSPECTOR: And who might you be?

ALBERT: A good friend of the family. A family friend. But who might you be?

INSPECTOR: I'm Inspector Vermont.

ALBERT: Inspector? Something wrong?

INSPECTOR: A dead body.

ALBERT: How awful. How did it happen?

INSPECTOR: Poison.

ALBERT: People are very careless nowadays. You know, that really hits me. That man was a very good friend to me. I'm really moved, but it was to be expected. Lately he was very depressed. I hope his widow isn't too overwrought. An extremely sensitive woman. They loved each other very much. It must've been a severe blow for her.

INSPECTOR: A slight misapprehension, Mr. . . . eh . . . Mr. . . . .

ALBERT: Wester. Mr. Wester. You can call me Albert if you like.

INSPECTOR: As I said already, a slight misapprehension, Mr. Wester. It's not your friend the Professor we found dead here.

ALBERT: *(Severely shocked)* What did you say?

INSPECTOR: It was his wife.

ALBERT: His wife? That's impossible. I mean . . .

INSPECTOR: What do you mean, Mr. Wester?

ALBERT: *(Recovering)* I mean . . . I'm amazed. I could imagine him doing it. A sensitive man, and very melancholy. But she was always full of life.

(INSPECTOR *opens the door and gives a sign.* EWALD *and* HELEN *enter.* ALBERT *looks at them as if seeing ghosts, and then starts as if to flee)*

INSPECTOR: Will you be so kind as to stay here for a few minutes?

EWALD: This is the man who blackmailed my wife, Inspector.

ALBERT: How dare you! *(To* INSPECTOR*)* It's a lie.

INSPECTOR: The Professor states that she must've given you money, just yesterday.

ALBERT: That's a lie!

INSPECTOR: May I see your wallet for a minute? *(With a swift movement he takes Albert's wallet and checks the numbers of the bills inside against the numbers in his book)* You have no objection to my keeping them for awhile? Have you anything to say, Mr. Wester? The numbers match.

ALBERT: *(To* EWALD*)* You rat! And I trusted you and your words. You swindler!

INSPECTOR: The pot shouldn't call the kettle black.

ALBERT: Yes, I've taken money, but from him, not from her. And I will tell you why. I don't care who knows it. That fine

Professor, Inspector, is a thief. He stole the work of a dead colleague. *(Silence)*

INSPECTOR: Is that true, Professor?

EWALD: I don't understand what he's jibbering about.

ALBERT: I can prove it. *(To* EWALD*)* You thought that I gave you everything, didn't you? But I kept a photocopy. Here it is. Inspector, he's just a little, low-born hijacker who lifted his buddy's work.

INSPECTOR: *(Takes the photocopy)* Very interesting. I don't understand much of it. Is this your handwriting, Professor?

EWALD: Oh, yes.

HELEN: What does all this mean?

ALBERT: He's nothing but a crook.

INSPECTOR: *(To* ALBERT*)* How did you get that manuscript?

ALBERT: I happened to find it here.

INSPECTOR: *(To* EWALD*)* What kind of manuscript is this?

EWALD: A scientific joke.

HELEN: May I see it? *(Reads)* Derksen? Who's that?

ALBERT: That's a dead colleague of the Professor. He made a discovery which the Professor lifted. That's how he became a professor. It will stir up a nice scandal when it gets out.

HELEN: Who's Derksen? And what is the Harabolet mushroom?

EWALD: They don't exist at all.

INSPECTOR: Could you make yourself a little more clear?

EWALD: It's all very simple. A joke, perhaps somewhat childish, for the faculty magazine. You know how scientists are. For years they work on a very specialized subject, and then they are apt to lose their grasp of its relativity. For those who know,

I've made a parody on it. I invented a certain Professor Derksen who discovered a totally new mushroom. He uses a very special jargon, but just slightly exaggerated so that it becomes ridiculous. An innocent joke by a scientist who doesn't want to dry up in his specialty. That's all. I don't understand why this man saw an opportunity for blackmail here.

ALBERT: You lie. You were afraid I would let it out.

EWALD: But it's already been out for a long time. I've had it printed in the faculty magazine. Here it is. Read it yourself.

INSPECTOR: No, thank you, it's not my profession. I prefer to read a good detective story.

ALBERT: He lies. I've been paid for it.

EWALD: Yes, you have been paid for it, but not by me. You were paid by my wife. You blackmailed her just like you have blackmailed a lot of other women.

ALBERT: *(Desperately, to* INSPECTOR*)* He lies, Inspector, he's a liar!

INSPECTOR: If I were you, I wouldn't kick up such a fuss over a little blackmail.

ALBERT: What do you mean?

INSPECTOR: Somebody has been murdered in this room.

ALBERT: Murdered?

INSPECTOR: Yes. Professor Harewood's wife. Poisoned. With whisky.

ALBERT: And you said it was suicide.

INSPECTOR: I never said that. I couldn't have said it, either, for the simple reason that it was not suicide. It was murder.

ALBERT: What have I got to do with it?

INSPECTOR: Your fingerprints were on a sloppily cleaned glass, in which there were still traces of good whisky. Her finger-prints were on the glass with the poisoned whisky. You had a drink with her. You poisoned her liquor. She must have been deep in her cups, so it was an easy trick. Then you washed your glass. But not carefully enough. Fingerprints stick tight. And you left her glass on the table where you were both sitting. No wonder that you thought I talked about suicide. It looked a little bit like it. You laid the scene beautifully.

ALBERT: It's not true.

INSPECTOR: Fingerprints don't lie.

ALBERT: It can't be true. I didn't do it. Which glass was it? I have a right to see that glass. You can't accuse somebody of murder just like that.

INSPECTOR: This is the glass.

ALBERT: (Pointing to EWALD) That's the glass he gave me to drink whisky out of.

INSPECTOR: When?

ALBERT: When? Let me think for a moment. I'm a bit dizzy. Oh yes, now I know. When I—well, when I . . . when I told him that I had found the manuscript.

INSPECTOR: So he offered you whisky when you were blackmailing him?

ALBERT: Yes.

INSPECTOR: Well, professor?

EWALD: I never have whisky here, let alone the fact that I should have offered it to him during a discussion in which the symbol inherent in a shared drink would be so inappropriate.

ALBERT: But he has liquor here, Inspector. Now you can see how he's lying. He has hidden the whisky.

INSPECTOR: (Intensely) You know where?

ALBERT: (Screams) Yes!

INSPECTOR: I see. So you could find it immediately without losing time.

ALBERT: Yes!

INSPECTOR: Where?

ALBERT: Here, behind the books, behind Pope. Because nobody ever reads him. A whole bottle of whisky. *(Goes to the bookcase and pulls out the tomes of Pope. The* INSPECTOR *stands behind him)*

INSPECTOR: There's nothing.

ALBERT: But the bottle *was* here. *(He rummages through the bookcase)*

INSPECTOR: Come with me without trouble and try to find a good solution for a couple of problems that desperately need an explanation.

ALBERT: I didn't do it. He murdered her. *(Points to* EWALD*)*

INSPECTOR: Easy does it.

ALBERT: You swine! You ratted on me. But you won't get Albert. *(He flees through the garden door)*

INSPECTOR: He won't get far. I have some men outside.*(Takes his walkie-talkie)* Vermont here. Seize that man who's coming from the garden. Over. *(Listens)* All right. *(Puts the walkie-talkie away)* Well, that seems to me the end of the case. The fingerprints and the numbers on the bills are ample proof. The case is rounded off, and a rounded-off case is an agreeable case for a policeman. Goodbye, Professor. Perhaps you will be called as a witness. Goodbye, Miss Engels. *(Farewells, exits, silence)*

HELEN: So it's over.

EWALD: Yes.

HELEN: She wanted to poison you.

EWALD: Yes.

HELEN: And he poisoned her.

EWALD: Yes.

HELEN: He used a lot of poison. Far too much. It must've killed her immediately.

EWALD: He was always the kind of cowardly braggart. He had to be doubly sure with everything he did.

HELEN: It's a just ending.

EWALD: Yes.

HELEN: *(Embracing him)* Darling, we'll be very happy.

EWALD: Yes. *(Disentangles himself)* And now you must let me alone.

HELEN: I want to stay with you.

EWALD: Go to the lab. The work must go on. I'll be with you in an hour.

HELEN: *(Kisses him)* Good. But not later.

EWALD: I promise.

(Exit HELEN. EWALD takes the manuscript from his desk and slowly tears it into pieces. The garden door opens and the COMMERCIAL TRAVELLER enters.)

CT: I waited till you would be alone.

EWALD: We don't have much to discuss any more.

CT: Everything has gone according to plan, I presume?

EWALD: Yes.

CT: You had no difficulty getting rid of the whisky?

EWALD: No. When we arrived here this morning, I asked Helen to wait for a few moments at the front door. During that time I flushed the whisky away and put the bottle in the neighbor's garbage can near the back alley, at the end of the garden, just like you told me to. The only flaw was that the body was lying near the bookcase. I had to carry it to the table.

CT: As you see, no more than a few minutes' work. You must admit I was right. It really was all very simple.

EWALD: Yes. I admire your ingenuity.

CT: It's my profession. Now we only have to settle the bill. When can that be?

EWALD: As soon as I get the money from the insurance company.

CT: Fifty thousand, isn't it?

EWALD: Yes, my wife and I took out the same Insurance at the same time.

CT: Then you owe me twenty-five thousand. Fifty percent. The normal rate.

EWALD: That's all right.

CT: Good. Some people object to paying when the work has been completed. I don't think that's very sensible.

EWALD: You'll get what we have agreed upon, to the last penny. I don't myself want to profit from that money. I'll give it to a scientific institution. I don't want to take any advantage from the death of this unhappy, unlucky woman.

CT: She deliberately tried to murder you. Twice, even. For she, nor her admirable lover could know that the mushroom he found in your room, with such a detailed description of its venomous qualities, was a perfectly edible and innocent Mirabellus and not a Pseudo.

EWALD: How could you foresee that everything would happen as it did? That all the culprits would get their punishment?

CT: A matter of arrangement. That's my profession. It has all been planned with regard to the nature of the participants. They had to act as they did. By the way, it was not his intention to poison her, but you. On my instigation he put poison in the whisky on the assumption that you alone made use of that bottle. I prepared it all very carefully, as I said, in accordance with the situation, the characters involved, and the evidence I had against them.

EWALD: But how?

CT: A matter of organization and resources. Don't you worry about that. It was all a part of the picture that I advised you to show Mr. Wester that bottle behind Pope and to give him a drink so that his fingerprints would be on the glass.

EWALD: And why did you advise me to let myself be blackmailed with that sham manuscript?

CT: As another proof of his guilt. After all, he did commit that murder, although it was not his intention.

EWALD: Couldn't you have invented a more simple plan?

CT: No. Imagine, Professor, that I had come to you with the proposition of doing away with your wife for you. How would you have reacted?

EWALD: *(After deep reflection)* I would have refused.

CT: Of course. Your conscience would have spoken. Very unbusinesslike, but very humane. When I gave you the proof however, with the sham Pseudomirabellus, that your wife was willing to participate in poisoning you because this greedy young man had come into her life, and when it became clear that these two people would not stop with one attempt, then you were ready to help justice have its own way. Both of them had your annihilation in mind. They destroyed each other. It's a nice example of earthly justice. That's our profession. It requires months of preparation, but in such a way that those involved remain ignorant of it.

EWALD: Everything is very clear now.

CT: A fine case. I've worked on it with pleasure. Good craftsmanship. A case with an artistic touch. That gives satisfaction. Any more question?

EWALD: No, thank you. I know enough.

CT: Then I'll say goodbye now. I wish you much happiness, Professor. *(Exit)*

(EWALD looks after him for a long time. Then he leaves too. The sound of his car is heard. Immediately afterwards HELEN enters. She beckons through the garden door. Enter COMMERCIAL TRAVELLER)

HELEN: It's over.

CT: A fine piece of business.

HELEN: Yes.

CT: He's irrevocably trapped.

HELEN: Yes.

CT: A highly distinguished man. One of our finest experts in the field of painless and untraceable poisons. How far is he with his investigations?

HELEN: He's nearly finished them.

CT: He'll be very useful to us. With this poison at our disposal, with this laboratory, and with a professor who has to obey us, we can corner the greatest part of the homicide industry on the world market.

HELEN: Perhaps it will be more difficult to force him to cooperate than I thought. He's very soft, but at the same time very stubborn.

CT: He will have to.

HELEN: Yes. In the long run he will have to. With the evidence we have against him.

CT: *(Embraces her)* Good work. And now off to the lab. Perhaps you can start preparing him for what's cooking for him. I think it's too cruel to permit him a taste of happiness before the truth grabs him by the throat.

HELEN: Yes, I'll tell him today. *(Embraces CT)* I don't like men who smoke pipes. They stink of old age. *(Exit both)*

(After HELEN *and* CT *have left the room, the* INSPECTOR *enters, carrying a whisky bottle wrapped in a handkerchief. He speaks into a walkie-talkie)*

INSPECTOR: This is Inspector Vermont. Seize the girl and the man coming out of the garden now. The case is finally closed. Over. *(Listens)* Yes, the Professor made one mistake. This Mr. Wester, that ratty crook, had thrown half the bottle of poison into the whisky, probably to be more sure than necessary, all in line with his character. That must've caused immediate death. The victim could never have made it to the table. She must've dropped dead right on the spot, where we found the traces of whisky. This Mr. Wester was right. There was whisky behind Pope. It must've been disposed of, bottle and all, within a space of, let's say, one or two minutes. I've checked it. There's only one excellent, obvious and yet unobtrusive hiding-place, where I found the bottle, indeed. In the neighbor's garbage can. The Professor's fingerprints are still on it. Over. *(Listens)* No, no, that's a job for Henderson. I want to sleep, do you hear me? I'm going home, and for twenty-four hours I don't want to hear about any murder whatsoever.

[THE END]

A play about Benjamin Franklin in Paris. To be produced by
CSC Repertory in New York in the Winter of 1983.

A three-character romance set in an electrical workshop. Produced at St. Clement's in New York in the Spring of 1981 and an upcoming production at the CAST Theater in Los Angeles in the Winter of 1983.

ESCOFFIER

KING OF CHEFS

by

Owen S. Rackleff

A one-man show about the legendary chef. Produced at St. Clement's in New York in the Spring of 1981.

LOOKING–GLASS

by Michael Sutton and Cynthia Mandelberg

A play about the life of Lewis Carroll with fantasy sequences that take place in ALICE IN WONDERLAND. Produced at the Entermedia Theater in New York in the Spring of 1982.

SOME RAIN

by James Edward Luczak

A three-character play, lyric realism, about loneliness. Produced at the Eugene O'Neill Playwrights Conference in the Summer of 1982 and on Theater Row in New York in the Fall of 1982.